Getting Skills Right: Assessing and Anticipating Changing Skill Needs

Please cite this publication as:
OECD (2016), *Getting Skills Right: Assessing and Anticipating Changing Skill Needs*, OECD Publishing, Paris.
http://dx.doi.org/10.1787/9789264252073-en

ISBN 978-92-64-25206-6 (print)
ISBN 978-92-64-25207-3 (PDF)

Photo credits: Cover Cell phone: © Creative Commons/Alfredo Hernandez, clock: © Creative Commons/Hakan Yalcin, cloud upload: Creative Commons/Warslab, join: © Creative Commons/Tom Ingebretsen, doctor: © Creative Commons/Joseph Wilson, chef: © Creative Commons/Alfonso Melolont

Corrigenda to OECD publications may be found on line at: *www.oecd.org/about/publishing/corrigenda.htm*.

Foreword

Across countries, substantial changes in skill needs are challenging labour market and training policies and contributing to skill mismatch and shortages. In most countries, large shares of employers complain that they cannot find workers with the skills that their businesses require. At the same time, in many countries, a number of college graduates face difficulties in finding job opportunities matching their qualifications.

In light of these challenges, OECD has undertaken an ambitious programme of work on how to achieve a better alignment or skill supply and skill demand, with a focus on: i) understanding how countries collect and use information on skill needs; ii) investigating cost-effective training and labour market policies to tackle skill mismatch and shortages; iii) studying the incentives of training providers and participants to respond to changing skill needs; and iv) setting up a database of skill needs indicators.

This work builds on the extensive programme of work of the OECD in the area of skills, including the OECD Skill Strategy and its follow up national studies, the Survey of Adult Skills (PIAAC) and its rich analytical programme, and several studies in the areas of skills mismatch, vocational education and training and work-based learning.

The present overview report identifies effective strategies for turning qualitative and quantitative information on skill needs into relevant policy actions. It provides a comparative assessment of practices in 29 countries in the following areas: the collection and use of information on skill needs to foster a better alignment of skills acquisitions with labour market needs; and the use of effective governance arrangements to ensure good co-ordination across the key stakeholders in this area. The assessment is based on the results of a questionnaire that was sent out to countries as well as analysis of other relevant information on practices.

The work on this report was carried out by Fabio Manca and Guillermo Montt in the Employment Analysis and Policy Division of the Directorate for Employment, Labour and Social Affairs, under the supervision of Glenda Quintini (Skills Team Manager) and Mark Keese (Head of the Employment Analysis and Policy Division). The report benefited from helpful comments provided by the following colleagues from the Directorate for Employment, Labour and Social Affairs: Stefano Scarpetta (Director), Mark Pearson (Deputy Director) and Stijn Broecke. Project assistance was provided by Natalie Corry. The care and effort taken by respondents to the survey sent to each country is greatly appreciated.

This report was produced with the financial assistance of the European Union Programme for Employment and Social Innovation "EaSI" (2014-2020) – grant number VS/2015/0372. The opinions expressed and arguments employed herein do not necessarily reflect the official views of the OECD member countries or of the European Union.

Table of contents

Figures

Tables

Executive summary and key findings

Skill mismatches and shortages are common in advanced economies. Many workers believe they have the skills to cope with more demanding work while some think they need more training to cope well with duties. On average, more than 40% of European workers feel their skill levels do not correspond to those required to do their job, with similar findings for Mexico, Japan and Korea. In parallel, many employers report that they face recruitment problems due to skill shortages.

Some degree of misalignment between the supply and demand for skills is inevitable, particularly in the short run. However, the costs of persistent mismatches and shortages are substantial. For instance, skill shortages can constrain the ability of firms to innovate and adopt new technologies while skill mismatches reduce labour productivity due to the misallocation of workers to jobs. Individuals are also affected as skills mismatch can bring about a higher risk of unemployment, lower wages, lower job satisfaction and poorer career prospects.

Policy intervention can help address skills mismatches and shortages but doing so successfully relies on having good information on current and future skills needs. This report identifies effective strategies for turning qualitative and quantitative information on skill needs into relevant policy actions. It provides a comparative assessment of practices in the following areas: the collection of information on existing and future skill needs; the use of skill needs information to guide policy development in the areas of labour, education and migration; and the existence of effective governance arrangements to ensure good co-ordination among the key stakeholders in the collection and use of skill needs information. The report is based on the results of a questionnaire that was sent to countries as well as analysis of other relevant information on practices. The following key findings emerge from the analysis:

- *Systems and tools for assessing and anticipating skills needs exist in all countries, but approaches vary significantly* in terms of: how they approximate skill needs (either by measuring specific skills directly or by using proxies such as qualification levels and vocational orientation, fields of study, or occupations); their time span (i.e. short-, medium- or long-term needs); their methods (one or several quantitative or qualitative sources); and their national/regional/sectoral scope. The most common approaches include medium-term occupational forecasts or assessments of current skill needs inferred from labour market information or vacancy surveys. In many countries, more than one exercise is carried out as each approach/method presents its specific advantages and disadvantages. For instance, Canada carries out analyses of existing skill shortages along with medium to long-run forecasts to identify future skill needs and imbalances. This enables the government to tailor immediate policy intervention (e.g. identify migration opportunities or develop short-term worker training schemes) as well as long-term policy orientations (e.g. develop apprenticeship programmes in certain fields).

- *Skills challenges are common to several policy domains, thus information on skill needs has the potential to inform various policy dimensions* and contribute to developing a systematic and comprehensive policy response to imbalances.
  - In employment policy, skill needs information is commonly used to update occupational standards, and to design apprenticeships, re-training courses and on-the-job training programmes. For example, in Australia, Belgium and New Zealand, skill needs information feeds into the National Occupation Standards to facilitate the rapid development of standards in new occupations or in occupations with changing skill requirements. In Turkey, these exercises are used to design apprenticeships in occupations and industries where shortages are identified. Also, in France, Hungary, Ireland and Italy, skill needs information is used to help in the transition to a greener and digital economy.
  - In education policy, skill needs information is commonly used to inform curriculum development and set the number of student places at all levels of education, including technical and vocational education and training (TVET) programmes. It also feeds into career guidance to inform students' choice.
  - In migration policy, skill needs information is used to fast track workers with skills that are in high demand. In Australia, analyses of job vacancies and contacts with employers contribute to identify occupations in current and future shortages in order to facilitate migration of workers with the relevant skills. Similarly, the United Kingdom's Migration Advisory Committee uses general labour market information to identify occupations experiencing shortages and advise the government on immediate skill needs.
- *Two broad challenges need to be overcome to ensure that information on skills needs is used more widely and effectively.* First, the characteristics of the exercises are often not aligned with the potential policy uses: the way skills are defined may not map on to useful policy-making variables, the output may be too technical, or the results may not be sufficiently disaggregated at the regional, sub-regional or sectoral levels. Second, the key stakeholders may not be sufficiently engaged and, when they are, disagreements about skills needs and the required policy response arise, requiring consensus-building. Some countries seem to do better than others in finding solutions to these challenges. For instance, the strength of Norway's skills assessment and anticipation system lies in that employment and education authorities are jointly involved in the design and development of the forecasts carried out by Statistics Norway, which ensures that they understand the outputs and use them for policy making.
- *Linking these exercises to more specific policies may help to overcome some of these challenges, but at the risk of losing wider relevance.* User/policy-driven exercises are narrower in scope as they are geared to very specific policy objectives and carried out by the end users of the information (e.g. public employment services in Austria, Belgium, France, Poland, Sweden and Turkey carry out skills assessment and anticipation exercises to inform their policies and programmes).
- *Information about skills needs is most effectively used in policy making when there is good co-ordination across ministries and strong stakeholders' involvement.* Effective collaboration usually involves clear leadership and allocation of responsibilities amongst those involved, as well as the engagement

of organisations that are representative of their base (e.g. sectoral organisations, trade unions or employer organisations). A variety of mechanisms have proven successful in helping to reach consensus, including working groups (e.g. the inter-ministerial skills working groups in United States), or round tables with specific objectives and timelines (e.g. in the Netherlands where they are successfully used to enhance collaboration across regional/sub-regional administrative levels). Sector skills Councils (e.g. in Canada, the Czech Republic and the United Kingdom) and independent bodies such as national skills advisory groups (e.g. in Denmark, Finland and Germany) can also improve co-ordination.

Chapter 1

Skills shortages and mismatches

Increased globalisation and rapid technological change, but also demographic, migration and labour market developments, have altered considerably the structure of skill requirements in most countries in recent decades – and these trends are expected to continue in the foreseeable future. In such a rapidly changing world, the need for the assessment of existing skill shortages and for forward-looking information on how the labour market and the demand for skills might change has become increasingly acute. Indeed, this chapter demonstrates that: i) the costs of "getting it wrong" are substantial, with significant economic costs, for individuals, employers, as well as society as a whole; and ii) the extent of mismatch and perceived shortages is high, and in some countries even increasing. Yet differences in the extent of mismatch and the prevalence of shortages across countries suggest that skills policies can make a difference.

The statistical data for Israel are supplied by and under the responsibility of the relevant Israeli authorities. The use of such data by the OECD is without prejudice to the status of the Golan Heights, East Jerusalem and Israeli settlements in the West Bank under the terms of international law.

In response to past and current changes in the types of skills needed, countries from around the world are increasingly paying attention to skills shortages and mismatches (ILO, OECD and World Bank Group, 2014). Stakeholders and businesses recognise that better aligning education and workforce needs is a top policy priority (TÜSIAD, 2014). In fact, job creation in Europe and the United States up to the 2020s will be largely driven by growth in high-skilled occupations. In Europe, this will mainly occur in professional services, business services and computing. It has been projected that 3 million new professional jobs will be created and over 5 million new technician and associate professional jobs. These trends require an up-skilling of the workforce: 19.4 million new jobs will require high-level qualifications which compensate for a declining number of jobs requiring medium- and low-level qualifications (EU Skills Panorama, 2014a). In the United States, employment growth is projected to be fastest in the healthcare, healthcare support, construction and personal care fields. Nineteen of the 30 occupations projected to grow fastest require post-secondary education, with the fastest growth projected among those jobs requiring a master's degree (Richards and Terkanian, 2013).

This chapter reviews the evidence on current skills imbalances. It sets the scene and provides background for a discussion of the policy avenues to address changing skill needs and frames skills assessment and anticipation exercises as a tool for countries to respond to them.

Main findings

- Skills mismatch implies costs for workers, employers and the economy. For workers, it brings about lower wages and lower job satisfaction. For the economy, it entails lower economic output. Skills shortages increase hiring costs and lower productivity.
- More than 40% of workers in Europe and other OECD countries like Japan, Korea and Mexico feel their skill levels do not correspond to those required by the job. Three out of ten workers believe they have the skills to cope with more demanding work and more than one out of ten believe they need more training to cope well with duties. Employers in most countries report difficulty in filling jobs, suggesting that the skills they require are not available in the labour market.
- Mismatch by field of study is the most common form of mismatch, followed by qualification mismatch. Although some level of mismatch is always to be expected, countries differ in the incidence of mismatch, suggesting that policies can make a difference.
- Several policy avenues exist to respond to skill shortages and mismatches. Skills assessment and anticipation exercises can provide evidence-based and reliable information to develop such policies.

The sources of skills mismatch and shortages

The past decades have seen an important shift in the types of jobs that make up the economy. Jobs are created and others destroyed, changing the skill demand of the economy. The skills required in the jobs that remain also shift, as the remaining jobs also change. These shifts have been brought about by, among other factors: changes in the global division of labour and a growing dependence of domestic jobs on economic globalisation; economic cycles and shocks; changes in the way firms are organised; technological innovation; demographic change; and changes in consumption models.[1] Rapid improvements in computer technology over the last few decades have provided employers with cheaper machines that can replace humans in many middle-skilled activities such as bookkeeping, clerical work and repetitive production tasks. Technology replaces certain tasks, changing the skill requirements to carry out a particular job. Improvements in technology enable employers to offshore jobs that do not require face-to-face interactions and shape a country's skills requirements. The pace of job technological job replacement seems to have slowed recently in the United States and there is debate as to how far this replacement will go (Autor, 2010, 2014; Bassanini and Manfredi, 2012; Cappelli, 1999). Countries and industries have shown a heterogeneous impact on wages and employment response to both the Great Recession and technological change (Eurofound, 2013a; Jaimovich and Siu, 2012). Economies' reaction to these changes depends, among other things, on their institutional and regulatory framework (Fernández-Macías, 2012).

The supply of skills is equally dynamic and has changed as a result of the expansion of compulsory and higher education (Meyer, Ramirez and Soysal, 1992; Schofer and Meyer, 2005), as well as changes in the quality of education (OECD, 2013b, 2013c), the increase in female labour force participation, migratory changes, demographic transitions, changes in the type of work carried out and the skills acquired as a result of experience, and changes in retirement regulation (Dixon, 2003; OECD 2013d, 2012a). Increases in skill supply can also be brought about by changes in the intensity (hours) or efficiency of work, potentially reducing shortages (Handel, 2012, 2003; Richardson, 2007).

The dynamism of both skill demand and supply raises the question of how economies match the two. In a perfectly competitive labour market, price and quantity adjust until the market clears: firms adapt production processes to the available stock of human capital and workers seek the amount and type of training currently required (or foreseen) in an economy (Hartog, 2000). This model relies on an assumption of perfect information. In reality, students, workers, employers and training institutions may not be well-informed about the skills required in the immediate-, medium- and long-term. In the presence of incomplete information, the time lag between the decision to enter education or a worker training programme and that of entering the labour market may lead individuals to under- or over-estimate employment prospects leading to mismatches and/or shortages. Workers may therefore have to accept posts for which they are mismatched, unless they go back in training to acquire the skill sets demanded by the economy; or employers invest in formal or informal training on-the-job. Similarly, when many of the attributes of the jobseeker are not easily observable to the employer, wages may not correspond to workers' productivity and may be unresponsive to changes in skills supply. As a result, lengthy periods of search might be required by both parties before job offers are made and accepted which means that overall mismatch can stretch considerably over time (Mortensen and Pissarides, 1999).

A lack of information is, therefore, an important driver of skill mismatch. Yet mismatch can still exist in the presence of perfect and complete information. Co-ordination failures can emerge when individual choices do not internalise other agents' preferences. Holzer (2013), for instance, suggests that students prefer education paths in fields where wages are expected to be high, not realising that other students will also have similar preferences and make the same investment, eventually overcrowding specific education fields. Further, for students and workers, financial constraints may limit the possibility of acquiring the skills in demand if individuals are unable to borrow (for lack of collateral), or lack sufficient savings to finance their up- or re-skilling (Bound et al., 2009; Haskins et al., 2009; Heckman and Lafontaine, 2007; Lovenheim, 2010). Equally, firms may not be in a position (or have the incentives) to adapt their productive processes to the available skill stock. Strict employment protection rules may make it costly for employer to hire workers with the skills required. It may make more sense to or retain mismatched workers and offer on-the-job training to employees lacking these skills. Also, some sectoral labour shortages may occur because the jobs on offer are not attractive enough to a sufficient number of people (e.g. resulting from long and anti-social hours, relatively low wages, or demanding working conditions) (EU Skills Panorama, 2014b).

National/local or individual financial and budget constraints may limit the ability to reduce mismatches and shortages. Tight budget constraints may lead some countries/regions to reduce their education and training offer and/or limit their ability of updating them with education programmes more in line with the skills required by the labour market. This situation can limit the availability of training opportunities, thus limiting students and workers' possibility of acquiring skills that are in high demand.

For all the above-mentioned reasons the market for skills is unlikely to clear (rapidly) in and of itself, and government intervention will be required to address these market failures.[2] As a consequence of the economic crisis, unemployment in the OECD has increased while some vacancies remained unfilled. In Europe, for example, unemployment rose from 7% in 2008 to 10.8% in 2013. Yet, in 2013, there were around 2 million vacancies available in the European Union and four out of ten employers reported difficulties in finding employees with the right skills. This indicates an imbalance between the available labour and the jobs in the EU labour market and shortages of the right skilled people in the right places to fill these vacancies (EU Skills Panorama, 2014b).

The economic costs of mismatch and shortages

Skills mismatch can have adverse effects both at the aggregate and individual levels. Total economic output at the aggregate level is influenced by how well workers are assigned to jobs, Mismatch results in economic output that is lower than the potential given by the economy's skills stock (Sattinger, 1993). Skill mismatches and shortages can negatively affect economic growth through their effects on: increased labour costs, lower labour productivity growth, slower adoption of new technologies, lost production associated to vacancies remaining unfilled, and the implicit and explicit costs of higher unemployment rates (OECD, 2012b). In particular, skill and qualifications mismatch is associated with lower labour productivity within industries (Adalet McGowan and Andrews, 2015). The aggregate costs of field-of-study and qualifications mismatch can amount to more than 1% of GDP due to losses in productivity and the sunk cost of developing skills that are not used (Mavromaras, McGuinness and Fok, 2009; Montt, 2015).

Skill shortages (particularly high-skill labour shortages) also have negative implications for the economy and the labour market. They increase hiring costs and lower productivity as vacancies remain unfilled for a longer period of time. Shortages can also induce wage inflation and, by increasing workers' bargaining power, raise demands for an easier pace at work. In an efficient labour market wages are indeed expected to rise in response to shortages, but persistent shortages and the consequent inflation can be a sign of skill supply not adapting to changes in demand. In addition, shortages can induce skills mismatch as workers from other fields seek employment in sectors experiencing shortages (Bennet and McGuinness, 2009; Haskel and Martin, 1996, 1993; Montt, 2015; Shah and Burke, 2005).

At the individual level, over-qualification and over-skilling entail lower earnings, lower job satisfaction and a higher risk of unemployment relative to well-matched workers. For example, over-qualified workers working in their field are expected to suffer an 18% wage penalty compared to well-matched workers; for over-qualified workers who are working in a sector or job unrelated to their field of study (i.e. field-of-study mismatch), this penalty amounts to 26%. Workers who were mismatched by field-of-study are also five percentage points more likely to be unemployed than previously well-matched workers (Montt, 2015; OECD, 2014).

In recognition of the costs of shortages and mismatches, the ability to assess and anticipate skill needs has become a notable policy concern across OECD and partner countries.[3] The 2008 International Labour Conference acknowledged that potential mismatch between skill demand and supply has high economic and social costs, contributing to structural unemployment (ILO, 2008). The World Economic Forum highlights the increased importance of matching skills and that skill mismatch has become more prominent during the last economic crisis (World Economic Forum, 2014). The G20 Training Strategy also recognises the importance of anticipating future skill needs (ILO, 2010).[4] Employment plans in G20 countries propose to address this challenge by promoting the collection and use of information on the demand and supply of skills, the transportability of educational and occupational credentials, the upskilling or reskilling of new, unemployed and displaced workers and the promotion of geographic mobility (ILO, OECD and World Bank Group, 2014).

Evidence of mismatch and shortages in selected countries

In the European Union, more than 40% of workers feel that their skill level is not matched to the requirements of the job; that is, workers have trouble finding jobs suitable to their skill levels. Similar estimates are observed in Mexico, Japan and Korea, with somewhat lower levels in Australia and New Zealand. In parallel, around 40% of employers report difficulties in recruiting staff with the right skills to perform the tasks required by the job; that is, employers have trouble finding workers meeting their skill requirements. The incidence of skill shortages and mismatches varies by country according to labour market conditions and the skills matching policies in place (Montt, 2015; OECD, 2013b; Quintini, 2011a; Wolbers, 2003). The level of skills shortage and mismatch may also differ across countries at different stages of economic development. Shortages are likely to be greater in countries with low educational attainment and high economic growth as their educational infrastructures may lag in adjusting to rapid structural change. On the contrary, in many developed countries, over-qualification or over-skilling may represent a common phenomenon as increasingly larger shares of youth graduate from tertiary education. As described below, high/low levels of skill mismatch and/or shortage speak to different labour market dynamics and therefore require different policy responses. Box 1.1 provides details on how skills shortages and mismatches are defined and measured.

Mismatch: Workers' perspective

Skills mismatch

This section estimates the extent of skills mismatch across a selection of OECD and European countries. Figure 1.1 shows that 45% of workers report experiencing skill mismatch in 2010 across the EU-27. They are workers who feel they lack the skills to perform their current job (i.e. under-skilled) or they feel they have the skills to perform more complex tasks (i.e. over-skilled). Self-reported mismatch was to highest in Romania, Greece, Hungary, Latvia, Slovenia and Albania, with more than 50% of workers feeling they are more (or less) skilled than what is required for the job. It was lowest in Lithuania, Belgium, Bulgaria, the Czech Republic, Finland, the Former Yugoslavian Republic of Macedonia (FYROM), Italy, Norway, Portugal and Turkey, at levels below 40%. In 2005, around 40% of worker-reported mismatch was observed for other OECD countries (Mexico, Israel and Japan) and 30% in Australia and New Zealand (Quintini, 2011a).

Box 1.1. **Defining and measuring skill shortages and mismatch**

Although there is no strict definition, skills mismatch and shortage describe situations in which workers' skills exceed or fall short of those required for the job under the current market conditions (Handel, 2003; Shah and Burke, 2005). More specifically, shortages occur when the skills sought by employers are not available in the pool of potential recruits. Mismatches, in turn, mean that workers are not well-matched with their current jobs. Mismatch implies that workers are either over-skilled, being able to deal with more complex tasks than those required by their jobs, or under-skilled and lacking the minimum skills required for their current jobs (OECD, 2014). Skill shortages can induce mismatch as employers, unable to find the skills needed, recruit mismatched workers.

Skill shortages can be measured in a variety of ways. For instance, vacancy surveys identify the skills that explain why posted vacancies remained unfilled after a certain period of time (see Box 3.1 for the use of such surveys in Australia and New Zealand). Shortages can also be assessed by indirect methods such as asking employers about the perceived difficulty for recruiting suitable workers or studying wage, employment and turnover trends in particular occupations in specific areas (Migration Advisory Committee, 2008).

Skills mismatches can be detected through surveys that ask workers whether they feel either over- or under-skilled for their current job (e.g. the European Working Conditions Survey). Other surveys, like the Survey for Adult Skills, measure three different types of mismatch: qualification mismatch, information-processing skill mismatch and field-of-study mismatch. In the case of qualifications mismatch, a worker has higher (or lower) qualifications than required to get the job. Alternatively, qualifications mismatch can be identified when a worker has a higher (lower) qualification level than the modal educational attainment for workers in the same job. Information-processing skill mismatch is observed when workers have better (or worse) numeracy or literacy skills than those possessed by workers who feel well-matched in the same job. Finally, in field-of-study mismatch workers received training in a specific field but work in an unrelated sector (OECD, 2014).

As developed further in Chapter 2, portraying an accurate picture of the level of skill shortages and mismatch across countries requires several simultaneous sources of information.

Source: Handel, M. (2003), "Skills Mismatch in the Labor Market", *Annual Review of Sociology,* pp. 135-165; Shah, C. and G. Burke (2005), "Skills Shortages: Concepts, Measurement and Policy Responses", *Australian Bulletin of Labour,* Vol. 31, No. 1, p. 44; Migration Advisory Committee (2008), *Identifying Skilled Occupations where Migration can Sensibly Help to Fill Labour Shortages,* London: The Migration Advisory Committee; OECD (2014), *OECD Employment Outlook 2014,* OECD Publishing, Paris, http://dx.doi.org/10.1787/empl_outlook-2014-en (accessed 8 February, 2016).

Not all types of skills mismatch are alike. For one, workers could be either over- or under-skilled. In general, workers were more likely to report being over- than under-skilled. On average across the European Union, 32% of workers report being over-skilled, having the skills to perform more complex tasks, while 13% report being under-skilled, requiring more training to perform their tasks (summing to a total of 45% of skill mismatch) (Figure 1.1). Comparing the rates of over- and under-skilling highlights how under-skilling is more of a problem in certain countries than in others. Under-skilling represents a more pressing challenge in Austria, Lithuania, Estonia, Germany and the Czech Republic where the percentage of under-skilled workers is comparatively close to that of over-skilled workers. By contrast, the bulk of the skills mismatch challenge relates to over-skilling in Romania, Montenegro, Greece, and Croatia. In these countries, fewer than 10% of workers report being under-skilled while more than 40% report being over-skilled. In these countries a considerable share of workers are employed in jobs that do not take full advantage of their skill set and human capital.[5]

Trends in skills mismatch

Between 2005 and 2010, the average EU-27 skill mismatch did not change (Figure 1.1). This average, however, masks important country-level variation over this period. Self-reported skill mismatch increased by more than one percentage point in eight of the 30 countries with comparable information (the Czech Republic, Greece, Latvia, Romania, Slovenia, the Slovak Republic and Spain). Skill mismatch decreased by more than one percentage point in 14 of the 30 countries, with the largest reductions observed in France (16 percentage points), Turkey (14 pp), Austria (11 pp), Ireland (8 pp) and Croatia (8 pp). When comparing the results for the year 2010 with those for 2005, the incidence of self-reported skills mismatch remained rather stable for those countries initially experiencing higher levels of mismatch (e.g. around 50%); it decreased for most countries where the percentage of mismatched workers was already low in 2005. This evidence could suggest the existence of specific weaknesses and gaps in the way some countries are able to match their stock of skills to their labour market demand and that such weaknesses do not appear to have been sufficiently dealt with over time.

Qualifications mismatch

Another way of measuring mismatch is through qualifications.[6] Workers can be over- (or under-) qualified for their job by having attained a higher (lower) educational level than that required by the job (or that commonly held by other workers in that occupation). Qualifications mismatch refers to the set of skills acquired in formal education. As a result, as workers gain work experience, their formal qualifications matter less – and so do the penalties related to qualifications mismatch. Qualifications mismatch is particularly relevant for youth as it sets out a career path that may lead to lower life-long earnings (OECD, 2014, 2015). Data from the European Labour Force Survey reveals that, in 2013 and across the EU-27, 23% of workers experienced qualifications mismatch with over-qualification being roughly twice as common as under-qualification. Qualifications mismatch was most common in Estonia, Greece, Ireland, Lithuania, Malta, Sweden and Switzerland. In these countries, more than 30% of workers experienced qualifications mismatch. Qualifications mismatch is least common in Croatia, the Czech Republic, Romania and the Slovak Republic (Figure 1.2).

Figure 1.2 also shows that, on average, qualifications mismatch in Europe does not seem to have changed substantially since 2006. It fell most notably in Iceland and Lithuania. It increased by more than 4 percentage points in Slovenia, Switzerland and the United Kingdom. Evidence from the academic literature, based on longer time series, suggests that qualifications mismatch has increased in recent decades in many countries. In Sweden, for example, workers in 1974 were over-educated by as little as half a year but average over-education increased steadily to almost two years in 2000 (Korpi and Tåhlin, 2009). Other European nations and the United States show similar long-term trends (Collins, 1979; Green, 2006; Vaisey, 2006).

Figure 1.1. **Skill mismatch in Europe**[a,b]

As a percentage of all employment

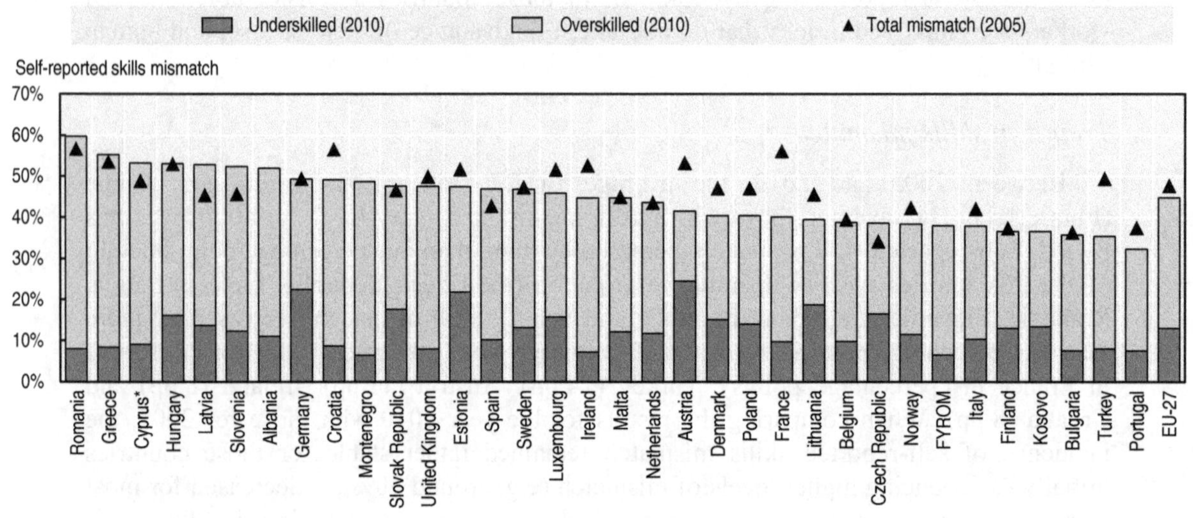

Countries are sorted by total skill mismatch.

a) Workers are classified as under-skilled if they report that they need further training to cope well with their duties or that they have the skills to cope with more demanding duties.

b) Total skill mismatch in 2005 is the sum of self-reported under- and over-skilled workers in 2005.

* Footnote by Turkey: The information in this document with reference to « Cyprus » relates to the southern part of the Island. There is no single authority representing both Turkish and Greek Cypriot people on the Island. Turkey recognises the Turkish Republic of Northern Cyprus (TRNC). Until a lasting and equitable solution is found within the context of United Nations, Turkey shall preserve its position concerning the "Cyprus issue".

* Footnote by all the European Union Member States of the OECD and the European Union: The Republic of Cyprus is recognised by all members of the United Nations with the exception of Turkey. The information in this document relates to the area under the effective control of the Government of the Republic of Cyprus.

Source: OECD calculations based on the European Working Conditions Survey (2010, 2005).

StatLink http://dx.doi.org/10.1787/888933333854

The estimates for qualifications mismatch in Figure 1.2 differ from those for skill mismatch in Figure 1.1. This is to be expected not only because one measure (overall skill mismatch) is based on self-reporting while the other is not. It is also expected because qualification mismatch is a form of mismatch that does not necessarily entail skill mismatch. Workers can be well-matched by qualifications but, because of skill heterogeneity within occupational groups, still feel mismatched. Alternatively, they can be mismatched by qualifications but have the adequate level of skills required for the job (Quintini, 2011b). Skill heterogeneity within an educational group is expected as graduates with a particular educational level differ in their skill levels (e.g. information processing, non-cognitive, job-specific or other types of skills).

Figure 1.2. **Qualification mismatch in Europe**[a, b]

As a percentage of all employment

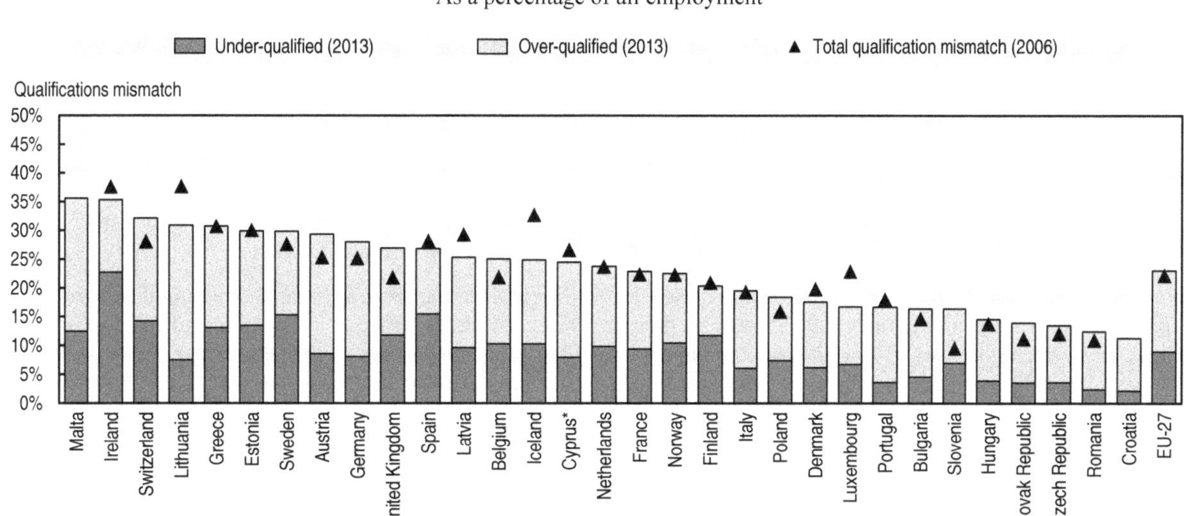

Countries are sorted the total qualification mismatch.

a) Workers are classified as under-qualified (over-qualified) if their educational attainment (four categories) is lower (higher) than the modal educational attainment of workers in their occupation within the country.

b) Total qualifications mismatch in 2006 is the sum of under- and over-qualification in 2006.

* See notes on Cyprus in Figure 1.1.

Source: OECD calculations based on the European Labour Force Survey (2013, 2006).

StatLink http://dx.doi.org/10.1787/888933333864

Mismatch: Additional evidence from the Survey of Adult Skills

The 2012 Survey of Adult Skills, the OECD's *Skills Outlook* (2013b) and the *Employment Outlook* (2014) examine different forms of mismatch: by qualifications, by information-processing skills and by field of study. Indeed, some workers may be over-qualified (or under-qualified) for their jobs. Others may be working in a sector of the economy (or job) that is unrelated to their field of study. And other workers still may be mismatched in a particular type of skill like numeracy if their ability to deal with numbers, calculation and other numeracy tasks exceed (or is insufficient for) those required by the job. (Box 1.2 provides more details on measuring these forms of mismatch in the Survey of Adult Skills.)

On average, across the countries that took part in the 2012 Survey of Adult Skills, 60% of workers are mismatched; they are either over/under-qualified, over/under-skilled or graduated from a field of study that is different from the job sector in which they work (field-of-study mismatch). While the sources and the magnitude of mismatches vary by country, over half of workers in 16 of the 22 countries are mismatched along at least one of these dimensions. Mismatch is most common in England/Northern Ireland (UK), France, Ireland, Italy, Japan, Korea, the Russian Federation and Spain, where more than three in five workers experience some type of mismatch (Figure 1.3). Mismatch is lowest in Finland, the Netherlands and Sweden, where fewer than 45% of workers experience one of these three types of mismatch.

Box 1.2. **Measuring qualification, skills and field of study mismatch in the Survey of Adult Skills**

Qualification mismatch arises when workers have an educational attainment that is higher or lower than that required by their job. If their education level is higher than that required by their job, workers are classified as over-qualified; if the opposite is true, they are classified as under-qualified. In the OECD Survey of Adult Skills, workers are asked what would be the usual qualifications, if any, "that someone would need to GET (their) type of job if applying today". The answer to this question is used as each worker's qualification requirement and compared to their actual qualification to identify mismatch. While biased by individual perceptions and period or cohort effects, self-reported qualification requirements along these lines have the advantage of being job-specific rather than assuming that all jobs with the same occupational code require the same level of qualification.

Skills mismatch arises when workers have a level of skills that is higher or lower than that required by their job. If their skill level is higher than that required by their job, workers are classified as over-skilled; if the opposite is true, they are classified as under-skilled (Krahn and Lowe, 1998). For the purpose of this chapter, skill requirements at work, the key term in the measurement of skills mismatch, are derived following Pellizzari and Fichen (2013).

Field of study mismatch arises when workers are employed in a different field from what they have specialised in. The matching is based on a list of occupations (at 3-digit of the ISCO classification) that are considered as an appropriate match for each field of study. Workers who are not employed in an occupation that is considered a good match for their field are counted as mismatched. The list of fields and occupations used in this chapter can be found in Annex 5.A1 of OECD (2014). The list is largely based on that developed by Wolbers (2003) but has been adapted to the ISCO-08 classification.

Source: Krahn, H. and G. Lowe (1998), "Literacy Utilisation in Canadian Workplaces", Catalogue No. 89-552-MIE, No. 4, Statistics Canada, Ottawa; OECD (2014), *OECD Employment Outlook 2014,* OECD Publishing, Paris, http://dx.doi.org/10.1787/empl_outlook-2014-en; Pellizzari, M. and A. Fichen (2013), "A New Measure of Skills Mismatch: Theory and Evidence from the Survey of Adult Skills (PIAAC)", *OECD Social, Employment and Migration Working Papers*, No. 153, http://dx.doi.org/10.1787/5k3tpt04lcnt-en; Wolbers, M. (2003), "Job Mismatches and their Labour Market Effects Among School-leavers in Europe", *European Sociological Review*, Vol. 19, pp. 249-266.

The most common form of mismatch is field-of-study mismatch alone (e.g. workers who are working outside their field but are not over- (or under-) qualified and have a level of skills adequate to the job) (dashed bar): on average across countries, 23% of workers are mismatched by field of study. When unaccompanied by over-qualification or over-skilling, field-of-study mismatch does not necessarily carry a wage penalty for workers, but does imply a loss in the investment made for field-specific training (Montt, 2015). Qualification mismatch, whether accompanied by field-of-study mismatch (dark blue) or not (light grey), accounts for around a third of overall mismatch. Over-qualified workers generally suffer an important wage penalty, implying important potential losses to productivity (OECD, 2014). Qualifications mismatch is notable in France and Japan, where more than 30% of workers are over-qualified within or outside their field of study; it is least common in Finland, Flanders (Belgium), the Netherlands and the Slovak Republic at less than 16%.

Figure 1.3. **Total mismatch, by type of mismatch**[a,b]

As a percentage of all employment

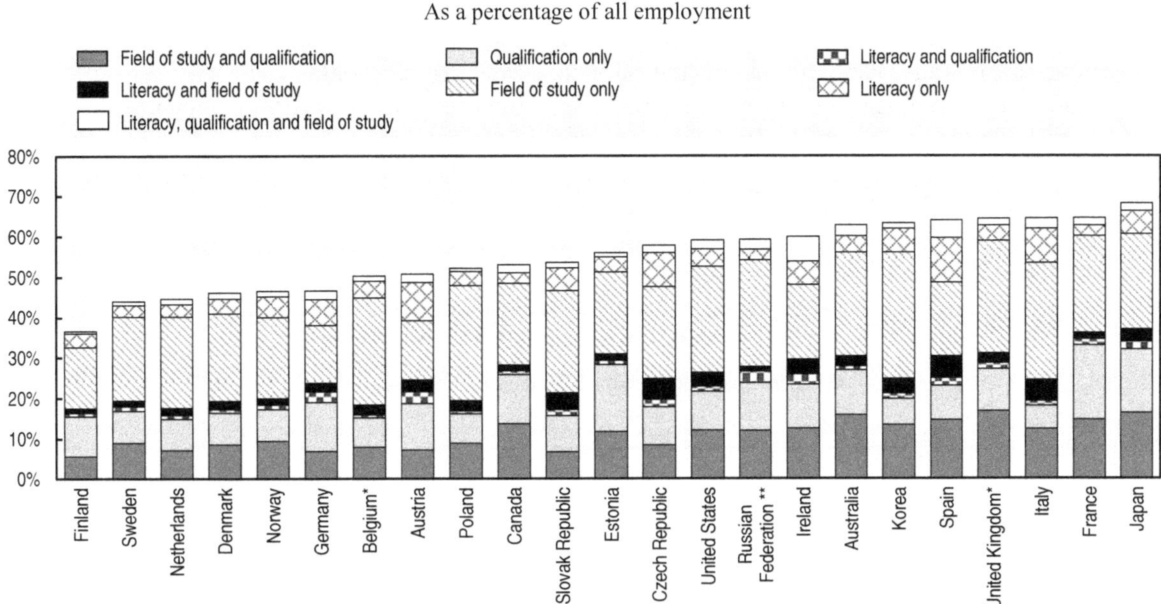

a) Workers are classified as mismatched by qualification if they have higher or lower qualifications than required by their job; workers are classified as mismatched in terms of literacy skills if they have literacy proficiency exceeding or below that required in their job; workers are classified as mismatched by field of study if they are working in an occupation that is not related to their field of study (see Box 1.2).

b) Occupation is only available at the 2-digit level in the ISCO-08 classification for Australia. It is not possible to assess the extent of field of study mismatch using the same definition used for the other countries.

* The OECD Survey of Adult Skills only covered Flanders (BEL) and England/N. Ireland (GBR).

** Readers should note that the sample for the Russian Federation does not include the population of the Moscow municipal area. The data published, therefore, do not represent the entire resident population aged 16-65 in Russia but rather the population of Russia excluding the population residing in the Moscow municipal area. More detailed information regarding the data from the Russian Federation as well as that of other countries can be found in the Technical Report of the Survey of Adult Skills (OECD, 2013b).

Source: OECD calculations based on the Survey of Adult Skills (PIAAC) 2012.

StatLink http://dx.doi.org/10.1787/888933333875

OECD findings further suggest that mismatch is common among all types of workers, although prime-age and older workers are less likely to be mismatched than young workers. Over-qualification related to field-of-study mismatch is, for example, almost twice more likely among young workers than among older ones. The likelihood of skills mismatch related to information-processing skills decreases as workers age. This is due, in part, to workers having had more time to find a job that matches their skills, but also to the fact that employers learn about workers' real skills which are not necessarily always aligned to their credentials or fields of study (OECD, 2014).[7]

Skill shortages: Employers' perspective

While many workers are over-qualified, over-skilled or working in a different field from that which they trained for, in 2013 around 40% of employers in Europe reported difficulties in finding employees with the required skills (Eurofound, 2013b). This experience of shortage is most (least) common in the manufacturing (financial) sector, and is also particularly common in Austria and the Baltic states (and least likely in Croatia, Greece or Spain). Another survey of more than 40 countries (both European and non-European) finds that 36% of employers find it difficult to fill specific vacancies. The biggest shortages are found in the skilled trades (e.g. welders, electricians and machinists), engineering and technicians.[8] More than half of managers in Japan, India, Brazil, Turkey and New Zealand report difficulties filling jobs (Figure 1.4). Fewer than 10% of firms report these difficulties in Ireland, the Netherlands, South Africa and Spain. Perceived shortages generally fell between 2007 and 2008 with the onset of the financial crisis, although they have increased again since 2008 despite persistently high levels of unemployment (Manpower Group, 2014).

Figure 1.4. **Skill shortage in selected countries**[a]

As a percentage of all firms with ten or more employees

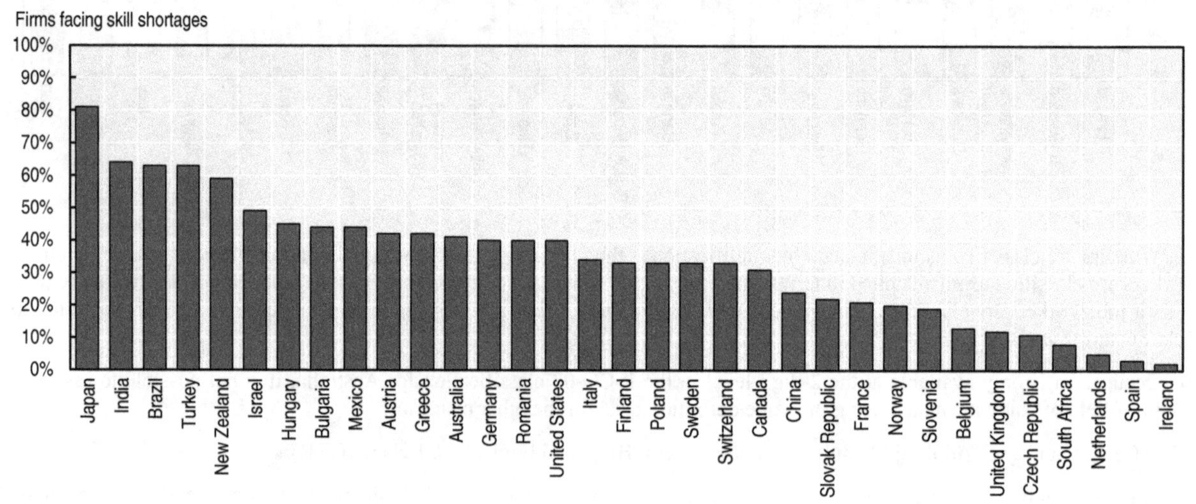

Countries are sorted by the total skill shortage.

a) Firms are classified as facing a skill shortage if their manager reports having difficulties filling jobs.

Source: Manpower Talent Shortage Survey (2014).

StatLink http://dx.doi.org/10.1787/888933333889

The challenge of skill shortage and/or mismatch

The facts that, on the one hand, a substantial part of workers are employed in jobs that do not correspond to their skill levels (Figure 1.1) and that, on the other, employers are not able to find workers with the skills they need (Figure 1.4), highlight the extent to which the labour market is unable to match the supply of, and the demand for, skills.[9] Aggregated data at the national level can hide even larger shortages and mismatches at the local level (Shah and Burke, 2005).[10] In many instances, labour markets can be localised at the sector, occupational and/or geographic level and an efficient allocation of skills to jobs will not work if both supply and demand are unresponsive to wages or to other employment conditions.[11,12] Thus, specific skill requirements at the sector level or the lack of geographic mobility[13] of jobseekers can reduce the scope for employers to find workers (and for jobseekers to find employment opportunities) and can exacerbate skill mismatches and shortages. In relation to geographic mobility, findings from the Netherlands show that mobile graduates are more likely to find jobs that are matched to their skills level (Hensen, De Vries and Cörvers, 2008). The fact that mobility reduces mismatch indicates that labour market shortages and mismatches are in some cases region-specific and could be alleviated by promoting geographical mobility in the labour market.

Countries can be located in a quadrant depending on the level of worker-reported mismatch and employer-reported shortage (Table 1.1).[14] Of the 24 countries with information on employer-reported shortages and worker-reported mismatch, Germany, Greece, Hungary, Japan, Romania and the United States can be classified as having a high level of mismatch (as perceived by workers) and a high level of shortage (as perceived by employers). For this group of countries, the policy challenges relate to the system by which workers are matched to jobs, the way skills are promoted by education and training institutions, how the development of these skills is aligned to those demanded by the labour market, the speed with which the provision of skills follows the changing demands of the labour market, or the transferability of a worker's skill set to different employers, occupations or economic sectors.

Table 1.1. **Skill mismatch and skill shortage in selected countries**

		Employer-reported skill shortage	
		High	Low
Worker-reported skill mismatch	High	Germany, Greece, Hungary, Japan, Romania, United States	Ireland, Slovak Republic, Slovenia, Spain, Sweden, United Kingdom
	Low	Austria, Bulgaria, Italy, Turkey	Belgium, Canada, Czech Republic, Finland, France, Netherlands, Norway, Poland

Note: A country is considered to have high (low) employer-reported skill shortage if it ranks in the top (bottom) half among countries in Figure 1.4. A country is considered to have high (low) worker-reported skill mismatch if it ranks in the top (bottom) half among countries in Figure 1.1. For Canada, Japan and the United States, the rank used for worker-reported skill mismatch is that of Figure 1.3. Only countries with results from the Manpower Talent Shortage Survey and either the European Working Conditions Survey or the Survey of Adult Skills are included. For those countries with data on both the European Working Conditions Survey and the Survey of Adult Skills, results from the European Working Conditions Survey are used in the classification.

Source: OECD calculations based on the European Working Conditions Survey (2010), Manpower Talent Shortage Survey (2014) and the Survey of Adult Skills (PIAAC) (2012).

StatLink http://dx.doi.org/10.1787/888933333904

Ireland, the Slovak Republic, Slovenia, Spain, Sweden and the United Kingdom, by contrast, can be classified as experiencing high levels of mismatch but low levels of shortage. For some of these countries it is also possible that educational expansion did not follow changes in labour market demand, and workers may have more than the skills required by employers. Another possibility is that employers in these countries recognise a broad set of skills as suitable for the job, but workers would like to have a better fit with their specific skills acquired through training. Finally, it may be that the economic crisis and low labour market demand has driven workers to accept jobs requiring different (and possibly lower) skills to the point that practically the few employers recruiting workers are able to fill their gaps.

In Austria, Bulgaria, Italy and Turkey, on the other hand, workers report low levels of skill mismatch, but employers report a high level of shortage. In this group of countries, it may be that the skills provided by education and training institutions are at a lower level than those required by employers. Finally, both shortage and mismatch are comparatively low in Belgium, Canada, the Czech Republic, Finland, France, the Netherlands, Norway and Poland. However, even if these countries seem to face lower levels of both mismatch and shortage than other countries, this does not mean that skills mismatches and shortages do not exist.

The responsiveness of skill supply to demand: An exploration by field of study

In a well-matched, efficient and effective labour market, skill demand and supply closely follow one another. The number of graduates from particular programmes should thus respond to employment prospects in the respective fields. Comparing graduation trends and employment prospects informs about the responsiveness of skill supply to skill demand. As mentioned earlier, mismatch results from imbalances labour demand and the skills produced in formal education and training; imbalances also occur as a result of changes in job characteristics and lags in workers' and employers' adaptation to these changes. The responsiveness of formal education to demand is only one indicator of a well-matched labour market.

In an efficient labour market, if the employment rate of a particular sector is lower than that of others, the number of graduates from the corresponding field of study should decrease. Similarly, if employment prospects for a sector are positive, the number of graduates from that respective field of study would be expected to increase to match the foreseen new vacancies. This would be the case if skills needs were adequately assessed and anticipated and stakeholders used this information to adapt and design policies to satisfy these needs (e.g. by better determining the provision of training offers or by providing information to prospective students).

Figure 1.5 shows, for each of eight fields of study[15] and for 26 European countries, the relationship between graduation rates and the relative employment rate of graduates from that field. On the vertical axis is the average growth in the number of young graduates from a specific field of study between 2006 and 2012, as a share of the total number of young graduates; and on the horizontal axis is the relative employment rate for graduates from that field in 2006. Ideally, graduation and employment rates would align on the top-right and bottom-left quadrants, meaning that graduation rates increase for fields of study experiencing better employment prospects (top-right quadrant) or that graduation rates decrease for fields of study experiencing low relative employment (bottom-left quadrant). The figure shows some, albeit very weak, signs of responsiveness of fields of study to labour market demand: those fields that increase (decrease) in size tend to be those where the relative employment rate was high (low). However, the great majority of fields appear to be unresponsive to employment prospects, as a large share cluster horizontally around zero. For those that do experience changes in graduation rates, many cluster vertically around one – i.e. the number of graduates changes, but not in response to the rather stable employment prospects.

Figure 1.5. **Change in the percentage of young graduates and relative employment rates across fields**

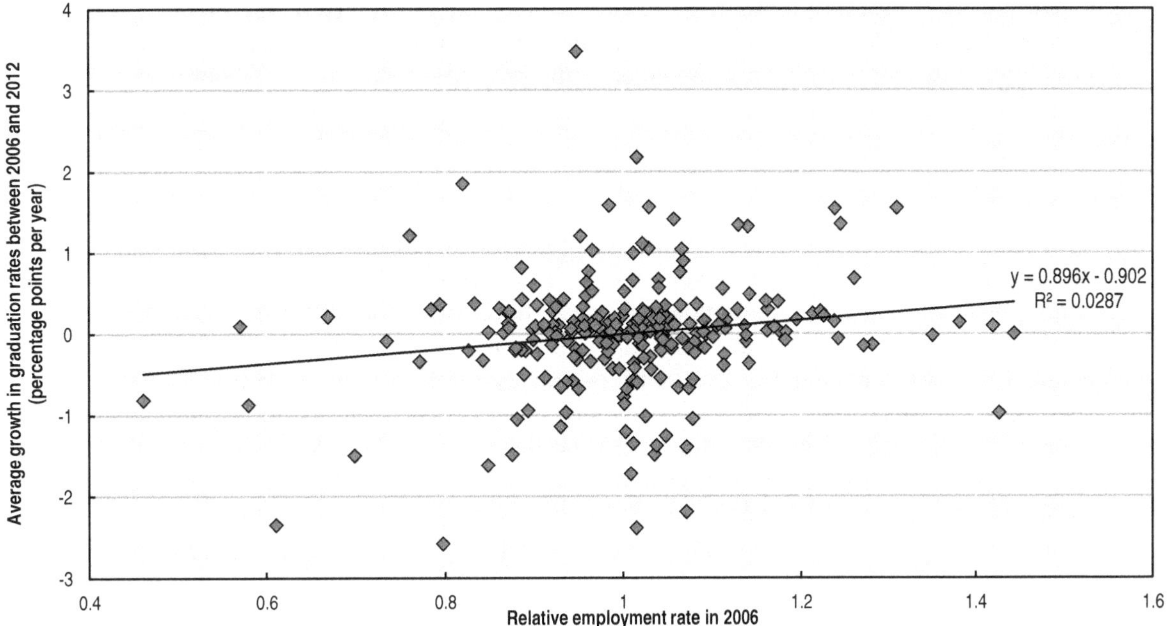

Note: The average growth in the percentage of graduates from each field is calculated over employed youth (aged 15 to 29) considering graduates from specific fields (i.e. excluding youth who graduated from "General Programmes") over the period 2006-12. The relative employment rate, considering the entire population, is calculated as the ratio of the employment rate for graduates from each field (irrespective of whether they work in the field or not) and the employment rate of the entire population. Relative employment rates above 1 mean that the employment rate among graduates from that field is higher than the national average; values below 1 mean that the employment rate for graduates from that field is lower than the national average. Each diamond represents one of eight fields in one of 26 countries.

Source: OECD calculations based on the European Labour Force Statistics 2006-2012.

StatLink http://dx.doi.org/10.1787/888933333890

Assessing and anticipating future skill needs to reduce skill imbalances

Despite the apparent inevitability of skills shortages and mismatches, several avenues exist to reduce their incidence. There is variability across countries in the prevalence of shortages and mismatches, indicating that they are sensitive to policy making and/or economic conditions. Indeed, specific policies – like those that promote mobility – can reduce shortages and mismatches. Quintini (2011b) suggests further policy avenues: improving career guidance services and the co-ordination between the labour market and the education system; increasing the offer for adult learning and work-based training or the training to unemployed workers; and evaluating rigid wage-setting institutions and employment-protection legislation that prevent wages and firms' employment from adjusting to mismatches.

Many of the solutions suggested by the existing literature to address skill shortages and mismatches involve the existence of information systems able to: i) assess the current and future supply of, and demand for, skills; and ii) to identify and/or anticipate skill shortages and mismatches (Shah and Burke, 2005).[16] Skills assessment and anticipation exercises (e.g. skill needs assessments, forecast and foresight exercises) can play a fundamental role in providing adequate information to relevant stakeholders to better plan the offer of education and training programmes in formal education and lifelong learning schemes and for individuals to decide on their future careers and work/education/training paths. These exercises do, in fact, exist in many countries. They highlight existing shortages or the skills needed in the medium- and long-term. They allow, at least in principle, to inform policies in accordance to the projected trends in the labour market by sector, region and/or occupation.

Conclusions

Increased globalisation and rapid technological change, but also demographic, migration and labour market developments, have drastically altered the structure of employment and the skill requirements of occupations in most countries in recent decades – and these trends are expected to continue in the foreseeable future. Such trends alter the demand for skills raising the questions of the extent to which economies face skill shortages and mismatches and how economies are able to match skill development to changing skill needs. Both the supply and the demand for skills are dynamic and they may well develop independently of each other as they respond to different drivers. It is no surprise, then, that skill mismatch and shortages are as common as they are – in fact, in the European Union, more than 40% of workers feel that their skill level is not matched to the requirements of the job and in many countries this figure is increasing – even though they bring about lower economic output for economies and lower pay and job satisfaction for workers.

Though seemingly inevitable, skill mismatches and shortages vary across countries, suggesting that they can be addressed through policy interventions. Skills assessment and anticipation exercises are policy tools countries can rely on to inform skill policies and reduce current or potential skill shortages and mismatches. Chapter 2 provides an overview of the different types of skills assessment and anticipation systems across some OECD countries and key partner economies.

Notes

1. See CEDEFOP (2008), Handel (2012, 2003), OECD (2013a) and Richardson (2007); and, for the well-documented processes of job polarisation, Autor (2010), Autor et al. (2003) and Goos et al. (2009).

2. Skills or labour shortages can be apparent or genuine. Apparent skills shortages occur when workers are unwilling to take up jobs given the current employment conditions; because skills are present but not put to use due to market factors, as wages and working conditions adjust, these skills shortages should disappear. Genuine skills shortages occur when vacancies remain unfilled despite attractive working conditions (OECD, 2012b).

3. Shortages and mismatch that require policy attention and can benefit from anticipation exercises are those that require long training periods, particular geographic mobility, or have restricted entry (restricted to license-owners or non-foreign workers). Shortages and mismatch in occupations that require low training periods may need less policy attention as they may be overcome by market forces (Shah and Burke, 2005).

4. In 2013, over half of the G20 member countries formally recognised the need to better align the supply of skills with the demand for skills in the context of changing skill needs (ILO, OECD and World Bank Group, 2014).

5. For some workers, mismatch is a voluntary outcome. It is conceivable that for many, however, it is a result of not being able to find a job that matches their skill set.

6. There are different ways to measure qualifications mismatch. Qualification mismatch based on self-reports usually ask workers about the qualification required to get their current job, and then compares that qualification with the qualification they actually hold. This is the measure of qualifications mismatch used in the Survey of Adult Skills (Figure 1.3). Another measure of qualifications mismatch is statistical: for each occupation, the modal educational attainment is compared to each worker's educational attainment. A worker with higher (lower) attainment than the mode for his/her occupation is considered over-(under)-qualified. This statistical approach is used to estimate qualifications mismatch from the European Labour Force Survey (Figure 1.2). Quintini (2011b) notes that statistical approaches to qualifications mismatch assume that all jobs with the same occupational title have the same educational requirements. They are also sensitive to cohort effects and to the level of aggregation to obtain a reliable distribution of education. In the estimates presented in this chapter, only occupations for which there are more than ten workers are considered. Estimates are country-specific so that educational requirements need not be identical across countries. These estimates are robust to an estimation that assumes variability in educational requirements by age groups (to account for cohort effects) but no variability across countries.

7. The finding that prime-age workers are less likely to be mismatched could also be due to age or cohort effects.

8. Although surveys to employers are a common way to detect shortages through reports of hard-to-fill or unfilled vacancies, employer reports of shortages often mask their unwillingness to offer competitive wages or working conditions or invest in worker training (Shah and Burke, 2005).

9. The contrasting experiences of skills shortage and mismatch experienced by employers and workers mirrors the discussion and treatment of skills mismatches in the academic literature and public opinion. While in the 1960s and 1970s academic attention focused on the increasing graduation rates and the failure of the economy to keep up to the populations' up-skilling, during the 1980s, 1990s and 2000s discussion shifted to the failure of graduates and the education system to keep up with economic transformations (Handel, 2003).

10. In fact, the more disaggregated the unit of analysis, the more likely it is to find shortages or mismatches, as they tend to offset each other in aggregated data (Shah and Burke, 2005).

11. Conditions of employment include, in addition to wages, burden of work, the quality of the working environment, prospects for mobility or career advancement, the commuting time and any other factor related to the job that jobseekers may consider when deciding to apply for a job or accept a job offer.

12. See, for example, Richardson (2007) for the use of skill needs information systems as a policy alternative in developing vocational education and training, and Spetz and Given (2003) and Shields (2004) in managing the supply and demand for nurses.

13. Results at the cross-national level will reflect those at the national, regional or local level if there was perfect information and geographic mobility across countries. The European Union, through the Employment Package is promoting free movement and a smoother flow of information through the European Network of Employment Services (EURES), the multilingual classification of European Skills, Competences,

Qualifications and Occupations (ESCO) and the portability of social security protection and pension rights for workers.

14. As mentioned in note 8, the validity and cross-national comparability of employer shortage reports can be low. Some of these concerns can be extended to worker self-reports of skill mismatch. As a result, the categorisation proposed in Table 1.1 should be taken with caution.

15. The eight fields of study analysed are: teaching, education and training: i) teacher training and education science; ii) humanities, languages and arts; iii) social sciences, business and law; iv) science, mathematics and computing; v) engineering, manufacturing and construction; vi) agriculture and veterinary; vii) health and welfare; and viii) services.

16. Also see, for example, Richardson (2007) for the use of skill needs information systems in the vocational education and training systems; and Ruhs and Anderson (2010) and Chaloff and Lemaitre (2009) in the development of migration policy. Chapter 3 of this report also develops the uses of skills assessment and anticipation exercises in the context of employment, education and migration policy.

References

Adalet McGowan, M. and D. Andrews (2015), "Labour Market Mismatch and Labour Productivity: Evidence from PIAAC Data", *OECD Economics Department Working Papers*, No. 1209, OECD Publishing, Paris, http://dx.doi.org/10.1787/5js1pzx1r2kb-en.

Autor, D. (2014), "Polanyi's Paradox and the Shape of Employment Growth", *NBER Working Paper*, No. 20485, Cambridge, United States.

Autor, D. (2010), *The Polarization of Job Opportunities in the US Labor Market: Implications for Employment and Earnings,* Center for American Progress and The Hamilton Project, Washington, DC.

Autor, D., F. Levy and R. Murnane (2003), "The Skill Content of Recent Technological Change: An Empirical Exploration", *Quarterly Journal of Economics,* Vol. 118, No. 4, pp. 1279-1334.

Bassanini, A. and T. Manfredi (2012), "Capital's Grabbing Hand? A Cross-Country/Cross-Industry Analysis of the Decline of the Labour Share", *OECD Social, Employment and Migration Working Papers*, No. 133, OECD Publishing, Paris, http://dx.doi.org/10.1787/5k95zqsf4bxt-en.

Bennett, J. and S. McGuinness (2009), "Assessing the Impact of Skill Shortages on the Productivity Performance of High-Tech Firms in Northern Ireland", *Applied Economics*, Vol. 46, No. 6, pp. 727-737.

Bound, J. et al. (2009), "Why Have College Completion Rates Declined? An Analysis of Changing Student Preparation and Collegiate Resources", *NBER Working Paper*, No. 15566, Cambridge, United States.

Cappelli, P. (1999), *The New Deal at Work*, Harvard University Press, Cambridge.

CEDEFOP (2008), "Systems for Anticipation of Skill Needs in the EU Member States", *CEDEFOP Working Paper,* No. 1.

Chaloff, J. and G. Lemaitre (2009), "Managing Highly-Skilled Labour Migration: A Comparative Analysis of Migration Policies and Challenges in OECD Countries", *OECD Social, Employment and Migration Working Papers,* No. 79, OECD Publishing, Paris, http://dx.doi.org/10.1787/225505346577.

Collins, R. (1979), *The Credential Society: An Historical Sociology of Education and Stratification*, Academic Press, New York.

Dixon, S. (2003), "Implications of Population Ageing for the Labour Market", *Labour Market Trends,* Vol. 111, No. 2, pp. 67-76.

Eurofound (2013a), *Employment Polarisation and Job Quality in the Crisis: European Jobs Monitor 2013*, European Foundation for the Improvement of Living and Working Conditions, Dublin.

Eurofound (2013b), *Third European Company Survey: First Findings*, European Foundation for the Improvement of Living and Working Conditions, Dublin.

EU Skills Panorama (2014a), *European Job Growth Creators Analytical Highlight*, prepared by ICF GHK and CEDEFOP for the European Commission.

EU Skills Panorama (2014b), *Skills Challenges in Europe Analytical Highlight*, prepared by ICF GHK and CEDEFOP for the European Commission.

Fernández-Macías, E. (2012). "Job Polarization in Europe? Changes in the Employment Structure and Job Quality, 1995-2007", *Work and Occupation*, Vol. 39, No. 2, pp. 157-182.

Goos, M., A. Manning, A. and A. Salomons (2009). "Job Polarization in Europe", *American Economic Review*, Vol. 99, No. 2, pp. 58-63.

Green, F. (2006), *Demanding Work: The Paradox of Job Quality in the Affluent Economy*, Princeton University Press, Princeton.

Handel, M. (2012), "Trends in Job Skill Demands in OECD Countries", *OECD Social, Employment and Migration Working Papers*, No. 143, OECD Publishing, Paris, http://dx.doi.org/10.1787/5k8zk8pcq6td-en.

Handel, M. (2003), "Skills Mismatch in the Labor Market", *Annual Review of Sociology*, pp. 135-165.

Hartog, J. (2000), "Over-Education and Earnings: Where Are We, Where Should We Go?", *Economics of Education Review*, Vol. 19, No. 2, pp. 131-147.

Haskel, J. and C. Martin (1996), "Skill Shortages, Productivity Growth and Wage Inflation", in A. Booth and D. Snower (eds.), *Acquiring Skills: Market Failures, their Symptoms and Policy Responses*, The Centre for Economic Policy Research, Melbourne.

Haskel, J. and C. Martin (1993), "Do Skill Shortages Reduce Productivity? Theory and Evidence from the United Kingdom", *Economic Journal*, Vol. 103, pp. 386-394.

Haskins, R. et al. (2009), "Promoting Economic Mobility by Increasing Postsecondary Education", *Economic Mobility Project*, Pew Charitable Trusts, Washington DC.

Heckman, J. and P. Lafontaine (2007), "The American High School Graduation Rate: Trends and Levels", *NBER Working Paper*, No. 13670, Cambridge, United States.

Hensen, M., M. De Vries and F. Cörvers (2008), "The Role of Geographic Mobility in Reducing Education-Job Mismatches in the Netherlands", *Papers in Regional Science,* Vol. 88, No. 3, pp. 667-682.

Holzer, H. (2013), *Skill Mismatches in Contemporary Labor Markets: How Real? And What Remedies*, Georgetown University and American Institutes of Research, Washington, DC.

ILO (2010), *A Skilled Workforce for Strong, Sustainable and Balanced Growth: A G20 Training Strategy,* International Labour Office, Geneva.

ILO (2008), *Conclusions on Skills for Improved Productivity, Employment Growth and Development: International Labour Conference*, International Labour Office, Geneva.

ILO, OECD and World Bank Group (2014), *G20 Labour Markets: Outlook, Key Challenges and Policy Responses*. Report prepared for the G20 Labour and Employment Ministerial Meeting, Melbourne.

Jaimovich, N. and H.E. Siu (2012), "The Trend is the Cycle: Job Polarisation and Jobless Recoveries", *NBER Working Papers*, No. 18334, Cambridge, United States.

Korpi, T. and M. Tåhlin (2009), "Educational Mismatch, Wages, and Wage Growth: Overeducation in Sweden, 1974–2000", *Labour Economics*, Vol. 16, No. 2, pp. 183-193.

Krahn, H. and G. Lowe (1998), "Literacy Utilisation in Canadian Workplaces", Catalogue No. 89-552-MIE, No. 4, Statistics Canada, Ottawa.

Lovenheim, M. (2010), "Housing Wealth and Higher Education: Building a Foundation for Economic Mobility", *Economic Mobility Project*, Pew Trusts, Washington DC.

Manpower Group (2014), Manpower Group Talent Shortage Survey 2014, Milwaukee: Manpower Group.

Mavromaras, K., S. McGuinness and Y. Fok (2009), "Assessing the Incidence and Wage Effects of Overskilling in the Australian Labour Market", *The Economic Record*, Vol. 85, No. 268, pp. 60-72.

Meyer, J., F. Ramirez and Y. Soysal (1992). "World Expansion of Mass Education, 1870-1980", *Sociology of Education*, Vol. 65, No. 2, pp. 128-149.

Migration Advisory Committee (2008), *Identifying Skilled Occupations Where Migration Can Sensibly Help to Fill Labour Shortages*, The Migration Advisory Committee, London.

Montt, G. (2015), "The Causes and Consequences of Field of Study Mismatch", *OECD Social, Employment and Migration Working Papers*, No. 167, OECD Publishing, Paris, http://dx.doi.org/10.1787/5jrxm4dhv9r2-en.

Mortensen, D. and C. Pissarides (1999), "New Developments in Models of Search in the Labor Market.", in O. Ashenfelter and D. Card (eds.), *The Handbook of Labor Economics, Vol. 3*, North Holland, Amsterdam.

OECD (2015), *OECD Employment Outlook 2015,* OECD Publishing, Paris, http://dx.doi.org/10.1787/empl_outlook-2015-en.

OECD (2014), *OECD Employment Outlook 2014*, OECD Publishing, Paris, http://dx.doi.org/10.1787/empl_outlook-2014-en.

OECD (2013a), *Interconnected Economies: Benefiting from Global Value Chains*, OECD Publishing, Paris, http://dx.doi.org/10.1787/9789264189560-en.

OECD (2013b), *OECD Skills Outlook 2013: First Results from the Survey of Adult Skills,* OECD Publishing, Paris, http://dx.doi.org/10.1787/9789264204256-en.

OECD (2013c), *PISA 2012 Results: What Students Know and Can Do (Vol. I)*, OECD Publishing, Paris, http://dx.doi.org/10.1787/19963777.

OECD (2013d), *International Migration Outlook 2013*, OECD Publishing, Paris, http://dx.doi.org/10.1787/migr_outlook-2013-en.

OECD (2012a), *Closing the Gender Gap: Act Now*, OECD Publishing, Paris, http://dx.doi.org/10.1787/9789264179370-en.

OECD (2012b), *Better Skills, Better Jobs, Better Lives: A Strategic Approach to Skills Policies*, OECD Publishing, Paris, http://dx.doi.org/10.1787/9789264177338-en.

Pellizzari, M. and A. Fichen (2013), "A New Measure of Skills Mismatch: Theory and Evidence from the Survey of Adult Skills (PIAAC)", *OECD Social, Employment and Migration Working Papers*, No. 153, Publishing, Paris, http://dx.doi.org/1787/5k3tpt041cnt-en (accessed 8 February, 2016).

Quintini, G. (2011a), "Right for the Job: Over-Qualified or Under-Skilled?", *OECD Social, Employment and Migration Working Papers*, No. 120, OECD Publishing, Paris, http://dx.doi.org/10.1787/1815199x.

Quintini, G. (2011b), "Over-qualified or Under-skilled: A Review of Existing Literature", *OECD Social, Employment and Migration Working Papers*, No. 121, OECD Publishing, Paris, http://dx.doi.org/10.1787/5kg58j9d7b6d-en.

Richards, E. and D. Terkanian (2013), "Occupational Employment Projections to 2022", *Monthly Labor Review*, December.

Richardson, S. (2007), *What Is a Skill Shortage?*, NCVER, Adelaide.

Ruhs, M. and Anderson, B. (eds.) (2010), *Who Needs Migrant Workers? Labour Shortages, Immigration and Public Policy*, Oxford University Press, Oxford.

Sattinger, M. (1993), "Assignment Models of the Distribution of Earnings", *Journal of Economic Literature*, Vol. 31, No. 2, pp. 831-880.

Schofer, E. and J. Meyer (2005), "The Worldwide Expansion of Higher Education in the Twentieth Century", *American Sociological Review*, Vol. 70, No. 6, pp. 898-920.

Shah, C. and G. Burke (2005), "Skills Shortages: Concepts, Measurement and Policy Responses", *Australian Bulletin of Labour*, Vol. 31, No. 1, p. 44.

Shields, M. (2004), "Addressing Nurse Shortages: What Can Policy Makers Learn from the Econometric Evidence on Nurse Labour Supply?", *The Economic Journal*, Vol. 114, No. 499, pp. 464-498.

Spetz, J. and R. Given (2003), "The Future of the Nurse Shortage: Will Wage Increases Close the Gap?", *Health Affairs*, Vol. 22, No. 6, pp. 199-206.

TÜSIAD (2014), *Business Priorities for Recommendations of Turkey's G20 Presidential Term in 2015*, TÜSIAD, Ankara.

Vaisey, S. (2006), "Education and its Discontents: Overqualification in America, 1972–2002", *Social Forces,* Vol. 85, No. 2, pp. 835-864.

Wolbers, M. (2003), "Job Mismatches and their Labour-Market Effects among School-Leavers in Europe", *European Sociological Review*, Vol. 19, No. 3, pp. 249-266.

World Economic Forum (2014), "Matching Skills and Labour Market Needs: Building Social Partnershisp for Better Skills and Better Jobs", *Global Agenda Council on Employment,* World Economic Forum.

Chapter 2

Tools and instruments to assess and anticipate skill needs

In this chapter, a comparative review is provided of the skills assessment and anticipation exercises currently in place in OECD countries. It explores the time span, the methods, the national/regional/sectoral scope and the skills definitions used. It shows that skills assessment and anticipation exercises are carried out in all countries, but that the approaches used vary. Current exercises are being developed further in many countries, with new exercises being developed in others. In most countries obstacles in the form of lack of funds or human resources with the relevant knowledge hinder the further development of such exercises.

Chapter 1 showed how, in most advanced economies, skill mismatches and shortages are relatively common. They result from the dynamism of both skill supply and skill demand. They also result from the unresponsiveness of skills development to the skills required in the labour market. Although skill mismatch and shortages are inevitable to a certain degree, the variability in shortage and mismatch levels across countries suggests that, for most countries, they could be reduced through policy. Many countries are, in fact, paying increased attention to developing mechanisms to better align skill demand and supply (ILO, OECD and World Bank Group 2014).

Drawing on previous reviews, available literature and responses to a purpose-designed questionnaire on anticipating and responding to changing skill needs (see Box 2.1), this chapter reviews skills assessment and anticipation exercises in place across countries. It identifies four dimensions (definitions, time span, methods and scope and coverage) to characterise the exercises. Any given exercise may focus on a particular time span and coverage, and use particular methods and definitions, depending on the objectives of the exercise and the available resources. Each approach has its specific advantages and limitations, which is one of the reasons why most countries carry out more than one skills assessment and anticipation exercise. The chapter also explores the reasons that hinder the further development of these exercises within countries, and highlights that most countries are developing new or strengthening current exercises.

Main findings

- Skills assessment and anticipation exercises exist in all OECD countries to identify current, short-, medium- or long-term skill needs. Many countries carry out different exercises (e.g. a current skill needs assessment and a medium-term forecast) as each approach has particular advantages and limitations.
- Most exercises approximate the measurement of skill needs through educational qualifications or fields of study. Several exercises measure occupational needs as a proxy to skills; some countries then link occupations to specific skill needs through occupational surveys. Only a few exercises measure specific skills directly (e.g. foreign-language skills, numeracy, co-operation).
- Most exercises rely on more than one method or data source, reducing potential biases and expanding the scope of the exercise. In most cases these are quantitative sources of information, though a few countries currently (and a few others will) systematically consider qualitative sources of information. Exercises can have a national, regional, or sectoral scope. Running specific exercises at different levels may risk producing inconsistencies or difficult comparisons.
- Skills assessment and anticipation exercises are being developed further in most countries, by refining the methodology, expanding the coverage of existing exercises or by creating new exercises altogether. Development is usually hindered, however, by lack of funds, lack of political support, lack of human resources with the relevant knowledge or poor statistical infrastructure.

What are skills assessments and anticipation exercises?

Skills assessment and anticipation exercises are tools to generate information about the current and future skills needs of the labour market (skill demand) and the available skill supply. Countries or regions can develop them to inform policies aimed at reducing skill mismatch and shortage. These exercises are not an attempt to plan the labour market from the top down, but a way to inform relevant stakeholders on how to better align the current and future supply and demand of skills in the context of rapidly changing economic conditions (Wilson and Zukersteinova, 2011). Skills assessment and anticipation exercises do not attempt to predict the future with certainty or precision. They are tools to help prepare or plan for future scenarios constructed from reliable evidence-based information (Wilson, 2012). Results from these exercises are intended to be an input for the discussion of policies between the various stakeholders involved in developing or implementing skills policies, not as the sole input in manpower planning techniques (Chapters 3 and 4).

Skills assessment and anticipation exercises have existed for more than 50 years. They take the form of occupational projections, specific skills assessments or other exercises. The Bureau of Labor Statistics in the United States, for example, began to include statistical projections in their 1960s *Occupational Outlook Handbook* (Rosenthal, 1999). Internationally, interest flourished in the 1960s following the OECD's Mediterranean Regional Project with the development of anticipation exercises in both developed and developing countries (Youdi and Hinchliffe, 1985). The availability of more and better information comparable across time and countries, and improvements in analytical tools, led to an increase in the number of countries implementing skills assessment and anticipation exercises over time. In Europe, the European Union and the European Centre for the Development of Vocational Training (CEDEFOP) have been instrumental in helping countries develop skills assessment and anticipation exercises (CEDEFOP, 2008a, Commission of the European Communities, 2009).

Box 2.1. **The Anticipating and Responding to Changing Skill Needs Questionnaire**

Recognising the potentially important adverse economic consequences of skill shortages and mismatch, the OECD in collaboration with European Centre for the Development of Vocational Training (CEDEFOP), the European Training Foundation (ETF) and the International Labour Organization (ILO) developed a questionnaire to identify effective strategies among countries for improving skills governance and turning qualitative and quantitative information on skill needs into relevant action for policy. A questionnaire was distributed to governments (Ministry of Labour and Ministry of Education) as well as to social partners (employer organisations and trade union confederations).

Replies from 29 OECD countries provide information on: the extent to which skills assessment and exercises, influence labour market, education and/or migration policy; the involvement of key stakeholders, including ministries of labour and education, local and regional authorities, employers and trade unions; and any good practice and/or barriers which are encountered in using such exercises in policy development. Annex A of this report summarises the responses received.

Skills assessment and anticipation exercises in OECD countries

Today, skills assessment and anticipation exercises exist in all OECD and European countries, although important differences exist in the approaches taken across countries, with exercises varying in terms of the *definitions* used for skills, the *time span* and *frequency*, the *methods* used and the *national/regional/sectoral scope*. To illustrate this variability, the Denmark Rational Economic Agent Model (DREAM) is a long-term dynamic computable general equilibrium model that can be used to simulate and forecast national education levels 50 or more years into the future (Rasmussen and Stephensen, 2014). Germany's BIBB-IAB-Qualification and Occupational Fields Projections develops 30-year forecasts occupations and qualifications drawing on both quantitative and qualitative data. Other exercises, by contrast, such as the Environmental Scans required by Industry Skills Councils in Australia, assess current skill needs in a particular sector of the economy drawing from interviews or focus groups with experts and actors involved in developing and using skills in that sector.

Definitions of skills used in the exercises

The term "skill" encompasses a wide range of attributes. It can refer to both generic skills and job/occupation/sector specific skills. Generic skills are those that are valued in every job, occupation and sector, and include cognitive skills such as information-processing skills (e.g. numeracy, literacy and problem-solving) as well as non-cognitive skills (such as perseverance, self-organisation, presentation, team-work and other such soft skills). Job-specific skills, by contrast, are not generally transferrable from one job/occupation/sector to another and refer, for example, to firm-specific knowledge about the functioning and culture of the organisation, technical knowledge, or practical competencies that are specific to a particular sector (e.g. manipulation of light pulses in the context of quantum optics, hairdressing, etc.).

Several challenges exist for skills assessment and anticipation exercises in relation to what is needed in the labour market. For the one part, many of these skills are difficult to measure, and, on the other, there may be no strict correspondence between how skills are understood in the skills development process (e.g. formal education credentials) and what is required in the labour market (e.g. specific occupations). Skill needs are commonly approximated by measuring which occupations are, or will be, in greater or lesser demand as they mirror economic projections. Given the need for planning in the education system, skills are also frequently approximated by qualifications (e.g. technical/vocational, university), fields of study (e.g. law, medicine, economics, catering) or, to a lesser extent, by measuring specific cognitive or non-cognitive skills (e.g. numeracy, literacy, soft skills, etc.).

As discussed in Chapter 3, a common obstacle in translating information from skills assessment and anticipation exercises to public policy is that the way skills are measured in such exercises does not translate easily into policy-making variables. To illustrate, exercises in several countries estimate which occupations will be in greater demand, but it is not always clear what skills, educational qualifications or fields-of-study are the most appropriate to satisfy those occupational needs. Similarly, exercises in several countries have identified "green jobs" as a key area of future skill needs, yet it is unclear what skills are entailed by such jobs. In some cases, where a qualifications framework, occupational standards or detailed descriptions about occupations exist, occupational needs can be linked to specific qualifications, fields of study or specific competencies to determine current or future skill needs in terms of attributes that are more useful to those responsible for designing skills policies.

In fact, exercises in relatively few countries assess or anticipate competencies directly. This is expected given that there are no agreed upon definitions of many of the myriad of job-relevant skills. Also, measuring them is costly and difficult. Canada's Office of Literacy and Essential Skills (OLES) is an exception. It funds projects that carry out skills needs assessments of generic skills, while matching resulting training interventions to employer demand. It has identified a set of Essential Skills, skills that are needed in nearly every job, with differing levels of complexity. OLES has developed descriptions of how these skills are relevant in each occupation. The set of Essential Skills includes: reading, writing, document use, numeracy, computer use, thinking, oral communication and working with others. In this context, OLES has funded a series of competency assessment tools, including the Test of Workplace Essential Skills (TOWES). Such competency assessment tools are most effective when individuals can assess and upgrade their skills in line with employer demand, as well as their own employment goals. The framework of Essential Skills and the TOWES has been used to inform the development of generic academic accreditation (e.g. ISCED 3 equivalent degrees for workers who did not finish upper secondary school). TOWES has been used in the province of Manitoba to identify generic skill shortages and inform curriculum development in adult training programmes.

Exercises in most countries measure skill needs in terms of qualification levels, qualification types or fields of study (Figure 2.1). One advantage of this approach is that these variables are more easily understood by a variety of stakeholders. Also, these variables are often readily available in existing datasets, facilitating the use of diverse and comparable information sources in skills assessments and forecast exercises. When Hungary surveys employers about their expected skill needs, these are expressed in terms of different educational attainment levels. Canada, for example, relies on administrative data for its Registered Apprentice Information System. Graduate surveys collect such variables as a matter of course, allowing policy makers to monitor potential mismatch between the outputs of the education system and the demands of the labour market. Canada also relies on forecasts from industry sector organisations such as *Buildforce Canada* for the construction sector in its efforts to anticipate and assess skill needs. In Canada, the majority of apprentices are found in the construction sector. Australia's Graduate Survey is one component of their skills assessment and anticipation exercises and both *Almalaurea*'s Survey on Graduates' Employment Conditions (Italy) and Norway's Candidate Survey (NIFU) contribute to assessing and identifying skill needs and their implications for education and training. The disadvantage of relying on measuring skills as qualification levels, types or fields of study is that educational credentials do not necessarily map to skills required on the job and that there is a substantial variability amongst individuals with the same credentials in terms of their skills and readiness to perform a job (Quintini, 2011).

Occupational forecasts are relatively common form of skills assessment and anticipation exercises. Skill needs assessment and anticipation exercises are usually linked to labour market needs, so they also proxy skill needs by the growth in specific occupations. Occupational forecasts are, in fact, at the origin of the skill needs exercises pioneered by the Bureau of Labour Statistics in the United States and the forecasting tradition of the Nordic countries. They project the changes in occupations using labour market and macroeconomic forecasts. Similarly, current skills assessments tend to focus on occupational changes, as is the case in the skill shortage lists developed in Australia and New Zealand.

Figure 2.1. **Measures used to assess or anticipate skill needs**

As a percentage of all countries

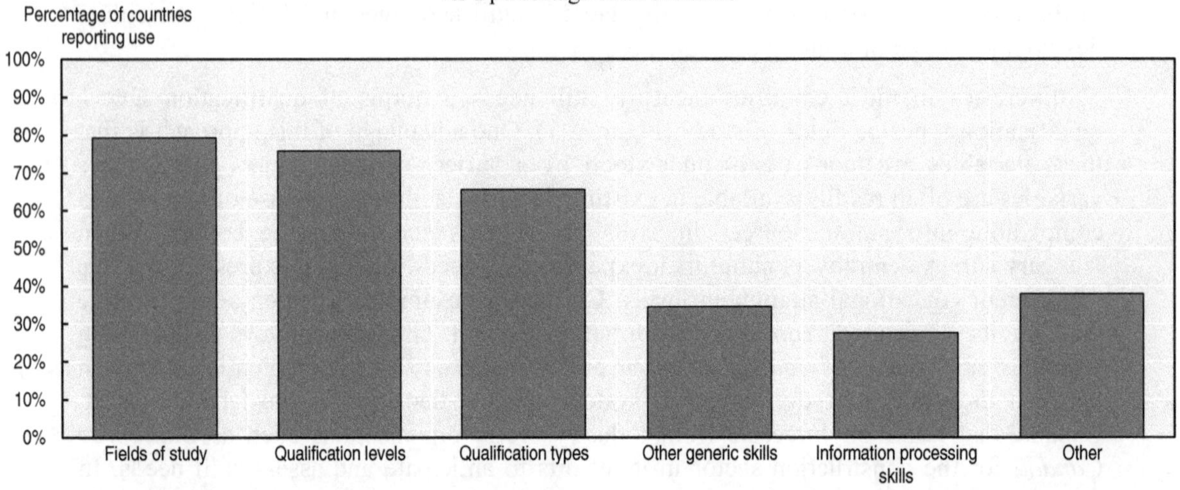

Note: Percentages based on responses from 28 countries (Australia, Austria, Belgium, Canada, Chile, the Czech Republic, Denmark, Estonia, Finland, France, Germany, Greece, Hungary, Ireland, Italy, Japan, Korea, the Netherlands, Norway, Poland, Portugal, the Slovak Republic, Slovenia, Spain, Sweden, Switzerland, Turkey and the United States). If more than one questionnaire was received per country, a definition is considered if reported in any questionnaire received.

Source: Questionnaire on Anticipating and Responding to Changing Skill Needs: Ministry of Labour and Ministry of Education questionnaires.

StatLink http://dx.doi.org/10.1787/888933333910

Exercises in several countries link occupation-based assessment and anticipation information to specific skills through comprehensive occupational standards or descriptions of what skills are required in each occupation. Canada's National Occupational Classification describes the world of work and occupations in Canada, including the skills required by each of 500 occupational unit groups. O*NET in the United States is a database containing detailed information about the knowledge requirements of more than 800 occupations. Following O*NET's model, and as part of the Occupations, Employment and Needs survey (*Professioni, Occupazione e Fabbisogni*), Italy carries out a survey to identify the skill, knowledge, values and attitudes required by an occupation as well as the work-style, general tasks and work-conditions commonly observed in each of 800 occupations (Castiglioni and Tijdens, 2014; ISFOL, 2014a). Users can then browse the employment outlook of each occupation, and link this outlook to the types of skills and knowledge which are (and will be) required by the labour market. In France, occupations are grouped into Professional Families (*Famille Professionnelle*). Each family groups occupations that call upon similar skills which are associated to particular qualification levels (DARES, 2009). Using the Professional Families, French policy makers can link trends in the demand for certain occupations to specific skill needs and educational credentials to inform the development of, for example, VET policy. Germany's BIBB-IAB-Qualification and Occupational fields follows 54 occupational fields and 63 industry sectors, which are linked to the exercises' monitoring of 5 different qualification levels.

Time span and frequency

A key distinction between skills assessment and anticipation exercises relates to the time span covered by such exercises. Exercises can either assess current skill levels and needs or anticipate future skill needs. Current skill needs assessments evaluate the current supply and demand for skills, with a particular focus on identifying mismatches or shortages. General Labour Market Information systems (LMI)[1] can be included under this heading, as long as they are used specifically to assess the relative supply of, and demand for, skills. The European Union, through Eurostat, carries out the Job Vacancies Surveys, providing quarterly and annual data on unmet labour demand in each member state. Anticipatory exercises look into the future, and can be further distinguished according to whether they are forecasts or foresight exercises. Forecast exercises use available information or gather new information with the specific aim of anticipating future skills needs, mismatches and/or shortages. Forecast results are meant to provide general indications about future trends in skill supply and/or demand in the labour market (CEDEFOP, 2008b). Foresight exercises provide a framework for stakeholders to jointly think about future scenarios and actively shape policies to reach these scenarios. Foresight involves stakeholders concerned with skills-related issues in a structured and constructive way to develop a common policy vision. Stakeholders develop priority-setting and are mobilised to translate it into policy action. A key distinction between forecast and foresight exercises is that the latter go beyond the exploration of future scenarios by promoting decision making and mobilising action to shape the future and realise these scenarios (ETF, 2014) (Table 2.1).

Table 2.1. **Skills assessment, forecast and foresight exercises**

Approach	Advantages	Disadvantages
Forecast-based projections and quantitative models at the national level	Comprehensive (typically, covers all sectors), consistent, transparent and explicit	Data demanding, costly; not everything is quantifiable and may give a false impression of precision/ certainty
Surveys of employers asking about skill deficiencies and skill gaps	Direct "user/ customer" involvement. Easy to set up and carry out	May be very subjective and inconsistent, with too much focus on marginal and ephemeral situations
Focus groups/round tables, Delphi style methods, scenario development	Holistic (considers a broader range of factors than just economic) Direct "use/customer" involvement	Can be non-systematic, inconsistent, and/or subjective
Sectoral/ occupational / regional studies and /or observatories (using both quantitative & qualitative evidence)	Holistic (for the sector). Partial (ignores other sectors). Strong on sector and other specific labour market dynamics	May introduce inconsistency across sectors

StatLink http://dx.doi.org/10.1787/888933333940

Most commonly, skills assessment and skills forecast exercises are carried out. Although skills foresight exercises are conducted in a large number of countries, they are, in comparison, less frequent (Figure 2.2). The existence of one type of exercise in a country (e.g. long-term forecasts) does not preclude the co-existence with another type (e.g. short-, medium-term forecasts, foresight exercises or current skills assessments). Each exercise may be designed to serve a different purpose and may be useful for different audiences, even if conducted by the same organisation. In fact, most countries have more than one skills assessment and anticipation exercise in place. Statistics Sweden has conducted short- and medium-term forecasts since 1959, but currently also conducts long-term forecasts covering a time span of 20 to 25 years. In addition, the Swedish Public Employment Service (*Arbetsförmedlingen*) carries out its own short-term forecasts to inform the development and targeting of their programmes. Australia has a well-developed system for assessing current skill needs and identifying shortages but also conducts independent occupational and sector-specific forecasts. Ireland conducts quantitative forecasts on-par with sector-specific foresight exercises. Germany complements its long-term forecasts (BIBB-IAB-Qualification and Occupational Fields) with short-term forecast exercises that feed specifically into the planning of vacancies in apprenticeships and a Foresight Initiative for Skill Needs (*Iniziative zur Früherkennung von Qualifizierungseforderníssen)*. Chile carries out regional forecast exercises and has begun to develop regional foresight exercises as well. In contrast, the Czech Republic, Estonia, Poland and Switzerland regularly conduct only one of these exercises in a regular manner.

Figure 2.2. **Use of current skills assessments, skills forecasts and skills foresight exercises**

As a percentage of all countries

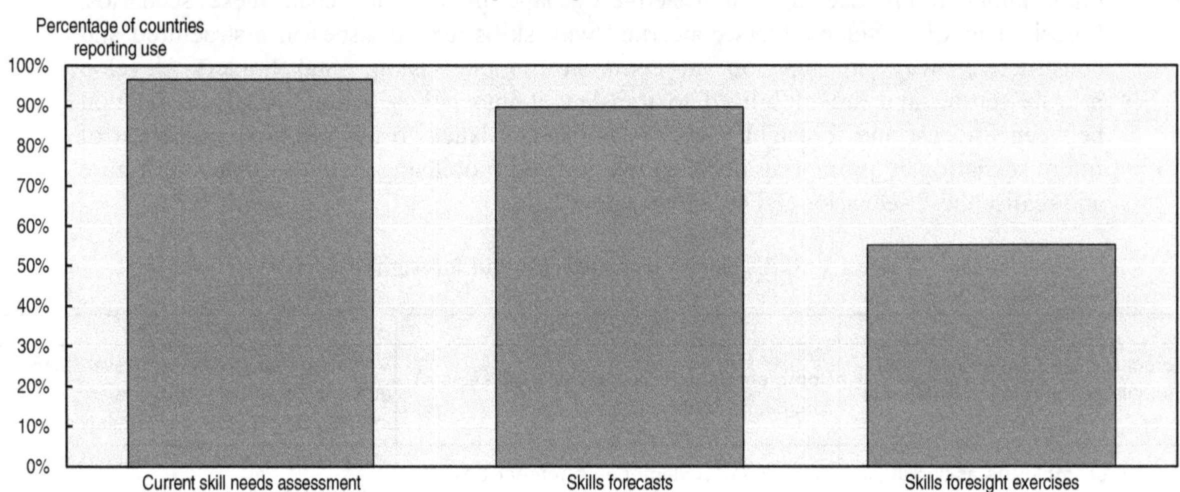

Note: Percentages based on responses from 28 countries (Australia, Austria, Belgium, Canada, Chile, the Czech Republic, Denmark, Estonia, Finland, France, Germany, Greece, Hungary, Ireland, Italy, Japan, Korea, the Netherlands, Norway, Poland, Portugal, the Slovak Republic, Slovenia, Spain, Sweden, Switzerland, Turkey and the United States). If more than one questionnaire was received per country, a use is considered if reported in any questionnaire received.

Source: Questionnaire on Anticipating and Responding to Changing Skill Needs: Ministry of Labour and Ministry of Education questionnaires.

StatLink http://dx.doi.org/10.1787/888933333929

Time span

Exercises specifically targeted at assessing current skill needs exist in practically all countries. In Australia and New Zealand current occupation- and region- specific shortages identified through vacancy surveys and other quantitative and qualitative methods (e.g. wage pressure analysis and feedback from employers). These shortages then inform migration and training policies. Japan's public employment agency (Hello Work) also relies on current skill needs assessments (by analysing job offers, job searches, outcomes of training and surveys of PES officials and employers) to identify skills in need and to develop re-training programmes. Current skill needs are also assessed by employer organisations, as is the case with the TEC Observatory

(*Observatoire Tendance Emploi Compétence*) in France, which collects information from firms on vacancies and recruitments to identify skills that are hard to find in the current labour market. This information is then used in discussions with government on education, migration and labour policy, or to develop training programmes for the organisation's members. Germany's Labour Market Monitor (*Arbeitsmarktmonitor)* reports every six months on the lack of professionals at the national and regional levels, without attempt to forecast future shortages directly.

Exercises to anticipate future skill needs can anticipate short- (6 months to 2 years), medium- (2 years to 5 years) or long-term scenarios (5 or more years). Most commonly, forecasts cover a medium-term time span, that is, they forecast skills needs and/or skills supply over a period of 2 to 5 years. Austria's AMS Qualifications Barometer provides forecasts of up to three or a maximum of 4 years (Humpl and Bacher, 2012). Long-term skill forecasts anticipate scenarios with a time span of more than 5 years; some produce scenarios 10, 30 or even 100 years into the future. Although expensive and requiring an important investment in statistical infrastructure, these exercises are also relatively common, particularly in the Nordic countries (Denmark, Finland, Norway and Sweden all have a tradition of producing long-term forecasts). Norway forecasts skill needs in the health sector 10 to 80 years into the future and needs in the teaching sector 35 years in advance. Norway also carries out 20-year general occupational forecasts. Denmark's DREAM model allows policy makers to evaluate future scenarios 100 years into the future (Rasmussen and Stephensen, 2014).

Short-term anticipation exercises are less common, perhaps because they differ little in purpose from the assessment of current skill needs. Poland's current or short-term skill needs are estimated by anticipating employment trends six months in advance. Norway estimates the education resources required one year in advance and also estimates employment trends in specific industries one year in advance as a direct input for planning training and employment policy in specific sectors, especially the public sector. The Italian Chamber of Commerce (*Unioncamere*) leads the Excelsior Project (*Progetto Excelsior*) which provides one-year forecasts of occupational changes (hiring and firing by firms across different sectors) based, in part, on surveys of employers regarding their hiring plans and short-term future skill needs.

As mentioned above, more than one exercise is usually used to identify current and future skill needs, usually because each exercise has its specific strengths and weaknesses and is best fit for a specific objective. Korea, for example, carries out different 1-, 3-, 5- and 10-year forecasts that are aligned to the respective national strategic development plans. Canada conducts short-, medium- and long-term forecasts. Long-term forecasts are useful exercises for medium-to longer-term planning, they require a more sophisticated statistical infrastructure because they require longer data time series and micro-data sources, and may entail an iterative validation process, which may not be easy to implement in all countries or regions. CEDEFOP's E3M3 forecast model, for example, draws on employment trends by economic sectors, national accounts, and economic and demographic projections (CEDEFOP, 2008b, 2012; Wilson, 2012). Long-term forecasts are also limited by the difficulty of estimating future skill demand, as the latter is sensitive to random shocks (e.g. unpredictable technological or economic change) (Wilson and Zukersteinova, 2011) – which reduces the reliability of such exercises. The perceived inaccuracy of long-term forecasts due to a lack of economic stability has hindered the development of such exercises in countries like Lithuania or those among the Baltic States (Martinaitis, 2012). On the other hand, while shorter-term forecasts and current skill assessments may provide more accurate scenarios, their policy usefulness may be restricted to short-term skills policies (e.g. migration, active labour market policies) but are limited in informing longer term education and vocational training policy as these programmes typically run over periods of two to five years.

Frequency

Current skills assessment and short- and medium-term forecasts are generally carried out (or updated) on an annual basis. Although long-term forecasts covering a time span of more than 10 years are run less frequently, they are still updated regularly to take into account new developments and ensure that the forecasts draw on the most up-to-date information on present and past trends. For example, Finland's long-term structural foresight exercise (VATTAGE) has a horizon of 15 years and is updated annually, while its qualitative exercise to anticipate competences and skill needs with a time horizon of 10 to 15 years is updated every four years. Finland's regional medium-term forecasts are updated twice a year.

Methods and data sources

CEDEFOP and the European Training Foundation (ETF) have reviewed the skills assessment and anticipation exercises in almost 30 countries. Exercises exist in all these countries, independent of the definitions used and their time span and frequency, they vary in the methodologies and data sources used (Bartlett, 2012; CEDEFOP, 2012, 2008b; Colicchio, 2012; Feiler, 2014; Lassnigg, 2012). Guidelines for the development of skills assessment and anticipation exercises highlight that they should adopt a *holistic* approach to measuring current or future skill needs. Exercises should be a "combination of various methods seeking to achieve robust and reliable results" (CEDEFOP, 2008a, p. 6). This combination incorporates, ideally, both quantitative and qualitative sources of information. Table 2.2 identifies the strengths and weaknesses of the different methods and tools to assess current and future skill needs. Exercises that adopt a holistic approach rely on a variety of methods, including (but not restricted to) macro-level forecasts, sectoral studies, questionnaires to employers and regional surveys on employment (CEDEFOP, 2008a, p. 25). The United Kingdom's sector-specific holistic approach to forecasting relies on econometric models, surveys of employers' opinions, skills audits, Delphi methods, case studies, focus groups, scenario development and consultation with experts and employers (CEDEFOP, 2008a, p. 7; UKCES, 2010).

Common quantitative sources of information include analyses of labour market information (e.g. flows in and out of employment by occupation and sector, trends in wages by occupation, trends in hours worked by occupation, etc.), vacancy surveys, employer surveys, surveys of recent graduates, and administrative data (e.g. data on enrolments in and graduation from various levels of education).

Each of these inputs serves a different purpose. For example, the United Kingdom's Migration Advisory Committee uses general labour market information to identify occupations experiencing shortages to advise the government on immediate skills needs that might be addressed through immigration policy (Migration Advisory Committee, 2008). New Zealand's vacancy surveys follow-up on posted vacancies to identify why certain vacancies remained unfilled (the Extensive Survey of Employers Who Have Recently Advertised). Employer surveys are used to ask employers about what they consider to be the skills currently in shortage (e.g. Manpower Talent Shortage Survey or Eurofound's European Company Survey). Hungary uses, employer surveys to identify what skills employers will need in the short-term future. Italy's survey of graduates analyses the employability of recent graduates to shed light on how well the education system is aligned to labour market needs. Administrative data are used in Canada through the Registered Apprenticeship Information System to monitor the intake and graduation from training programmes. Canada also relies on forecasts from industry sector organisations such as *Buildforce Canada* in its effort to monitor occupations experiencing shortages. In Germany, administrative data are used to monitor occupational trends through job openings notified to the German Federal Employment Agency, the registered unemployed and employees subject to social security contributions to estimate current occupational shortages.

Qualitative inputs include the industry round tables carried out within sector skills councils in Australia and the sector studies in Ireland's foresight exercises. They also include Delphi methods which, through iterative and anonymous participation from experts, allow reaching convergence on future scenarios (Mabotja, 2013) and scenario development (which are internally consistent views of a series of possible outcomes or scenarios of what the future may be; Wilson, 2012). Skills audits are also used in the context of Italy's *Professioni, Occupazione, Fabbisogni* (Occupations, Employment and Needs) foresight exercise (Castiglioni and Tijdens, 2014; ISFOL, 2014b). Germany's BIBB-IAB-Qualification and Occupational Fields long-term forecasts uses qualitative scenarios to contrast the baseline quantitative projections.

Table 2.2. **Advantages and disadvantages of skills anticipations methods and tools**

Approach	Advantages	Disadvantages
Forecast-based projections and quantitative models at the national level	Comprehensive (typically, covers all sectors), consistent, transparent and explicit	Data demanding, costly; not everything is quantifiable and may give a false impression of precision/ certainty
Surveys of employers asking about skill deficiencies and skill gaps	Direct "user/ customer" involvement. Easy to set up and carry out	May be very subjective and inconsistent, with too much focus on marginal and ephemeral situations
Focus groups/round tables, Delphi style methods, scenario development	Holistic (considers a broader range of factors than just economic) Direct "use/customer" involvement	Can be non-systematic, inconsistent, and/or subjective
Sectoral/ occupational / regional studies and /or observatories (using both quantitative & qualitative evidence)	Holistic (for the sector). Partial (ignores other sectors). Strong on sector and other specific labour market dynamics	May introduce inconsistency across sectors

Source: Adapted from Wilson et al. (2004).

StatLink http://dx.doi.org/10.1787/888933333957

Although adopting a holistic approach to assess current and future skill needs is considered good practice, in few countries exercises systematically combine quantitative and qualitative data sources in the same exercise. Australia, Flanders (Belgium), Italy and Korea are some examples where such exercises do.[2] In general, Italy's skills assessment and anticipation exercises are mostly quantitative (e.g. the *Fondazione Giacomo Brodolini*'s econometric model for the Italian Labour Market, FGB-LM model; Ciccarone and Tancioni, 2012), but the exercise that anticipates skills needs for professions and occupations (*Professioni, Occupazione, Fabbisogni)* relies on both a quantitative and a qualitative approach by combining labour market information, econometric forecasts, skills audits, scenario development and sector forecasts (Castiglioni and Tijdens, 2014).

Australia's current skill needs assessment draws on quantitative sources of information as well as on direct qualitative input from employers to identify occupations in shortage. Korea relies on both quantitative (LMI, employer and worker surveys), sector studies and other qualitative methods to develop their assessments and forecasts. Exercises in other countries draw on qualitative sources for validation purposes, not as an input in itself. The Canadian Occupational Projection System (COPS) forecasts and the Netherland's Research Centre for Education and the Labour Market (ROA) forecast are primarily quantitative, but rely on qualitative data sources as a second step to validate the quantitative forecasts. Finland and Estonia recognise the importance of qualitative input to their forecasts and plan to revise the methodology to better accommodate input from qualitative sources.

Many exercises rely solely on quantitative data, but draw on a range of different quantitative sources to identify current or future skill needs (Table 2.3). This is because relying on one source only limits the quality of the exercise, as is the case in Hungary which relies exclusively on employer surveys to identify current and short-term future skill needs. Results from such surveys may be biased by selective and/or low response rates and by the fact that employer reports of shortages often mask their unwillingness to offer competitive wages, competitive working conditions or training opportunities for workers (Shah and Burke, 2005). Similarly, relying only on labour market indicators, as is the case in Switzerland's national forecast and Chile's regional forecasts, reduces the scope of the forecast and limits the extent to which supply dynamics (e.g. migration, graduation trends) can be incorporated into the results. As a result of these method-specific limitations, and to increase the reliability of the exercises, they adopt a quantitative approach draw on information from different sources to inform their exercises.

A minority of exercises draw on qualitative data sources alone. These are usually foresight exercises, like Ireland's sector-specific foresight exercises and Australia's sector-specific Environment Scans.

As discussed in further detail in Chapter 3, an important set of barriers that prevent information from skills assessment and anticipation exercises from being translated into policy relates to the lack of consultation with stakeholders and experts in identifying skill needs, as well as the lack of consideration of key skill supply and demand dynamics. As recommended by CEDEFOP (2008), these barriers can be overcome with the adoption of a mixed methods and a holistic approach to the measurement of current and future skill needs.

Table 2.3. **Methods and tools used in skills assessment and anticipation systems**

	Employer surveys	Surveys of workers or graduates	Quantitative forecasting models	Sector studies	Qualitative methods	Labour market information system	Other
Australia	X	X	X	X	X	X	X
Austria	X	X	X	X	X	X	X
Belgium (Flanders)		X	X	X	X	X	
Belgium (Wallonia)				X	X	X	X
Canada	X	X	X	X	X	X	X
Chile	X			X	X	X	
Czech Republic			X	X			
Denmark	X	X	X	X	X		
Estonia			X				
Finland	X		X		X	X	
France	X	X	X	X	X	X	
Germany	X	X	X	X	X	X	X
Greece	X			X		X	
Hungary	X				X		
Ireland			X	X		X	
Italy	X	X	X	X			
Japan	X	X		X		X	X
Korea	X	X		X	X	X	
Netherlands	X		X	X	X	X	
Norway	X	X	X	X	X	X	X
Poland		X				X	
Portugal	X	X		X	X	X	
Slovak Republic						X	
Slovenia	X						X
Spain		X		X	X	X	
Sweden	X	X	X	X	X	X	
Switzerland							
Turkey	X	X		X	X	X	
United States		X	X		X	X	X

Note: Only the 28 countries or regions that replied to either the Ministry of Labour or the Ministry of Education are included. If a tool or method is mentioned in either questionnaire it is marked as used.

Source: Questionnaire on Anticipating and Responding to Changing Skill Needs: Ministry of Labour and Ministry of Education questionnaires.

StatLink http://dx.doi.org/10.1787/888933333964

National, regional or sectoral coverage

Finally, skills assessment and anticipation exercises can also differ in their coverage, as they can provide information about current or future skill needs at the national, regional or sector-specific level. Although national-level coverage may be useful for broad training policy and labour market monitoring, regional- and sector-specific exercises can facilitate more targeted policy making. In effect, labour market mobility often occurs within sectors or regions so mismatches and shortages observed in one region or level may not exist in others. National-level assessments or aggregate data may sometimes overlook specific skills needs that may be present in a particular region or sector (Shah and Burke, 2005).

To achieve national, regional and sectoral coverage, countries usually carry national assessments which allow for the disaggregation of results at the regional and/or sectoral levels. In other countries, a national exercise is complemented by independent regional or sectoral analyses, sometimes risking duplication or incomparability of results.

National-level skill needs assessment or anticipation exercises exist in practically all countries. Region-specific or sector-specific exercises are also common. Many times, region- or sector-specific exercises are integrated in the national-level exercises as national-level exercises frequently provide robust and valid information at the region or sector levels as well. For example, Poland's new national forecasting tool will provide forecasts to 2020 for the country as a whole, but also for occupational groups, economic sectors and regions separately. Austria's Qualifications Barometer information on current and short-term qualification needs for 24 sector/occupational categories, as well as for each of the nine regions (Humpl and Kargl, 2008). Analysing all three levels simultaneously may require large investments in statistical infrastructure. To reduce such burden, Finland's sector-specific analysis follows a rotating structure so that, in addition to the exercises providing information at the national or regional levels, sector-specific information is provided for two or three different sectors each year.

Other times, regional or sectoral analyses are carried out independently of the national analysis. In the United States the Bureau of Labor Statistics carries out national-level occupational demand forecasts and each region (state) also carries out their own, independent exercises to anticipate occupational demand within the state. In France, a national forecast is carried out jointly by the Prime Minister's office and the Ministry of Labour (*Prospective des Métiers et des Qualifications*, PMQ) while region-specific exercises are carried out by the regional development agency. In Switzerland and Norway, in complement to the national-level exercises, sector-level analyses are carried out by professional associations on an *ad-hoc* basis, as has been the case of skill needs assessments commissioned by the information technologies sector (ICT Switzerland), by the mechanical engineering sector (*Swissmem*) or by Norway's health care and educational sectors.

In some cases there is overlap between these exercises (e.g. Canada, France, Germany), in others there may be complementarity (e.g. Australia, Ireland, the United States), and in others, potential incompatibilities (e.g. Finland). In France, while there are national- and region-specific exercises, there is, at the same time, the public employment service's forecast (*Pôle Emploi*'s *Enquête Besoins en Main-d'Œuvre)* which provides skills needs assessments and projections at the national, regional and sector levels. In Germany, the long-term forecasts provide sector-specific results, yet sector-specific employer organisations also regularly carry out their own skills assessments. Australia's Skills Shortage Lists provides skill needs assessments at the regional and sub-regional levels (and at the metropolitan level for large cities) by identifying the occupations and sectors currently facing shortages. In addition, sector skills councils have the mandate to carry out environmental scans, which are mostly qualitative exercises to identify current and future skill needs – which also feed into the national Skills Shortage List. Ireland's national skills forecast is primarily a quantitative exercise, complemented by the qualitative sector-specific foresight exercises. In Finland, by contrast, the independent regional analyses are not harmonised in their methods and definitions, rendering comparisons and aggregations difficult or even impossible.

Table 2.4. **National, regional and sector levels covered in skills assessment and anticipation systems**

	National	Regional as part of the national	Independent regional	Sector as part of the national	Independent sector
Australia	X	X	X	X	X
Austria	X	X		X	
Belgium (Flanders)			X		X
Belgium (Wallonia)			X		X
Canada	X		X		X
Chile			X		X
Czech Republic	X	X		X	
Denmark	X	X		X	X
Estonia	X			X	
Finland	X	X	X	X	X
France	X	X	X	X	X
Germany	X	X		X	X
Greece	X				X
Hungary	X	X			X
Ireland	X	X		X	X
Italy	X	X		X	
Japan	X	X			
Korea	X	X		X	
Netherlands	X	X		X	
Norway	X	X	X	X	X
Poland	X	X			
Portugal	X	X		X	
Slovak Republic	X	X		X	
Slovenia	X	X			
Spain	X	X	X	X	
Sweden	X	X	X	X	X
Switzerland	X				X
Turkey	X	X		X	
United States	X	X	X	X	X

Note: Only the 28 countries or regions that replied to either the Ministry of Labour or the Ministry of Education are included. If a level is mentioned in either questionnaire it is marked as covered.

Source: Questionnaire on Anticipating and Responding to Changing Skill Needs: Ministry of Labour and Ministry of Education questionnaires.

StatLink http://dx.doi.org/10.1787/888933333975

The national level is less important, or altogether absent, in a few countries. In Belgium, labour market and education policy is the remit of each region – so skills assessment and anticipation exercises are not carried out at the national level, but by each region separately. In Hungary, the regional analyses are most important, and national-level results are produced as a second step in which regional-specific analyses are aggregated. In Germany, educational policy at the tertiary level is largely the remit of each *Lander*, increasing the relevance for the collection of region-specific skill needs information in the context of education policy. In Chile, there are no national level exercises and the most developed exercise is the annual mining-specific forecast carried out by the mining sector (*Consejo Minero de Chile*); Chilean regional exercises rely mostly on the analysis of labour market statistics and the regional foresight exercise is still in development. Up to now, all skills assessment and anticipation exercises were sectoral and carried out on an *ad-hoc* basis by sector organisations based on secondary data (LMI). A national Greek skills assessment and anticipation exercise is being developed by the Ministry of Labour and Social Solidarity in conjunction with the public employment service and the social partners. In Estonia, sector level forecasts are aggregated to identify national skill needs, and no regional-level forecasts exist. In the Slovak Republic, the most important exercises are also carried out at the sector level. Exercises are not carried out at the sector level in Japan, Poland and Slovenia.

Recent and ongoing developments

According to responses from the Anticipating and Responding to Changing Skill Needs Questionnaire, skills assessment and anticipation exercises are generally perceived to be reliable tools for identifying skills mismatches and imbalances, and most countries feel confident enough to use the information from such exercises to inform policies (see Chapter 3). In fact, there are plans in most countries to develop these exercises further in one way or another. In some places (e.g. Flanders [Belgium]), these new developments are the result of an increased interest in evidence-based policy making, giving skill needs assessments a greater role in the policy-making process.

In some countries, these developments are only a matter of refining existing methodologies. For example, and as mentioned above, Finland and Estonia are seeking to include more qualitative information into their forecasts. Switzerland will include more and better indicators to their current labour market forecasts, such as data on wages. Italy intends to explore new sampling criteria for their exercises to achieve better sectoral coverage. Korea plans to incorporate more contextual variables to ensure that national and international economic and social developments enhance the robustness of the results. Germany plans to forecast skill requirements rather than qualification types, thus better capturing specific employer demands.

In other countries the coverage of their current exercises is being expanded. Australia is exploring how to expand the assessment of current skill shortages to anticipate future ones. The Netherlands and Switzerland will refine the coverage of their current exercises to provide results with greater regional differentiation, while Italy will do so in order to increase sector coverage. Germany has recently begun forecasting at the regional level through the QuBE project and plans to improve the way the interaction between labour supply and demand are captured. Spain is expanding the experience of their Job Placement Survey of University Graduates to cover VET graduates with a new survey instrument.

Chile, the Czech Republic, Greece, France, Poland and Portugal are going further, and are developing new exercises. In Chile, regional foresight exercises are being developed by government agencies to contribute to regional development and entrepreneurship. The Czech Republic and Poland are replacing previous forecasts and assessments with entirely new exercises. In the Czech Republic, the "The Future of Professions" (*Budoucnost Profesí*) system of skill needs anticipation and forecasting was discontinued in 2012 and is being replaced by the "Skill Needs Anticipation" (*PŘEKVAP*) project. This new project (running over the years 2014 and 2015) will lay down the basis for a system of skills needs assessment and anticipation by improving the quality of the analytical tools and ensuring regular and long-term creation and use of skills needs information by the relevant stakeholders. A much more intense co-operation with employers is also envisaged through the already created sector councils. In Greece, the Ministry of Labour and Social Solidarity is leading the development of an integrated system to diagnose labour market needs and help employers in diagnosing and forecasting their own needs. This system is being developed with the involvement of the public employment service and the social partners. In Poland, the current skills assessment and anticipation initiative had been criticised by the employment service and labour offices because the inadequacy and imprecision of the indices and proxies used to quantify skills needs limited the use of the projections by relevant stakeholders. Thus, a new system of employment forecasts (*Prognozowanie Zatrudnienia*), co-funded by the European Social Fund, is being launched. Based on econometric forecasts, it projects employment demand to 2020 with the aim of informing public employment services and provide a reference point for labour market policy at the national, regional and local levels. In France, short-term skills forecasts are being developed to complement the medium- and long-term forecasts currently in place. Portugal has recently launched the *Sistema de Antecipação de Necessidades de Qualificações* (National Qualification Needs Anticipation System, SANQ). SANQ will identify short and medium-term skill needs at the regional level, set priority levels for qualifications and deepen the diagnosis of skill needs with stakeholders. SANQ receives the technical support of the International Labour Organisation (ILO).

Another line of development is in the way different skills assessment and anticipation exercises are articulated. France currently has a wide variety and large number of exercises carried out by: the Prime Minister's office and the research branch of the Ministry of Labour (*France Stratégie*, DARES), regional observatories (*Observatoire Régional Emploi Formation*, OREF), the public employment service (*Pôle Emploi*), the Centre for the Study and Research on Qualifications (*Centre d'Études et de Recherches sur les Qualifications*, CÉREQ), sectoral observatories and by employer organisations (e.g. MEDEF's *Tendance Emploi Compétence*). To better co-ordinate these different exercises and the information produced by each one of them, *France Stratégie* is developing an Employment Skills Network (*Réseau Emploi Compétences*, REC). Similarly, through a three-year project led by the Ministry of Education and Research, Norway is developing a national system for analysis, dialogue and dissemination of future skills needs. This system, led by the Ministry of Education and Research, will put together available analyses and statistics, identify knowledge gaps, and commission new analysis projects, such as foresight exercises.

Only Austria, Hungary, Ireland, Japan, the Slovak Republic, Sweden and the United States signal that there are currently no plans to further develop skills assessment and anticipation exercises. In Ireland, existing exercises are already judged to be effective tools to assess current and future skill needs. In Hungary, the absence of development relates to the fact that the legal framework governing Vocational Education and Training has only recently been established, and skills assessment and anticipation exercises are part of this legal framework – so new developments may still happen in the future.

Barriers to further development

In many skills assessment and anticipation exercises are being developed in one way or another. Notwithstanding their relevance and usefulness, several countries note that there are important barriers that hinder these exercises from being developed further (see Figure 2.3). Many identified the difficult co-ordination with relevant agencies [e.g. Canada, Chile, the Czech Republic, Flanders (Belgium), France, Italy, Portugal, Spain and Turkey] or the lack of political will as major obstacles [e.g. Flanders (Belgium), Portugal and Slovenia]. Others identified poor statistical infrastructure or a lack of human resources with the relevant knowledge and experience as a crucial factor hindering the development of skills assessment and anticipation exercises [e.g. Chile, Estonia, Ireland, Portugal, the Slovak Republic and Wallonia (Belgium)].

Figure 2.3. **Obstacles to the development of skills assessment and anticipation exercises**

As a percentage of all countries

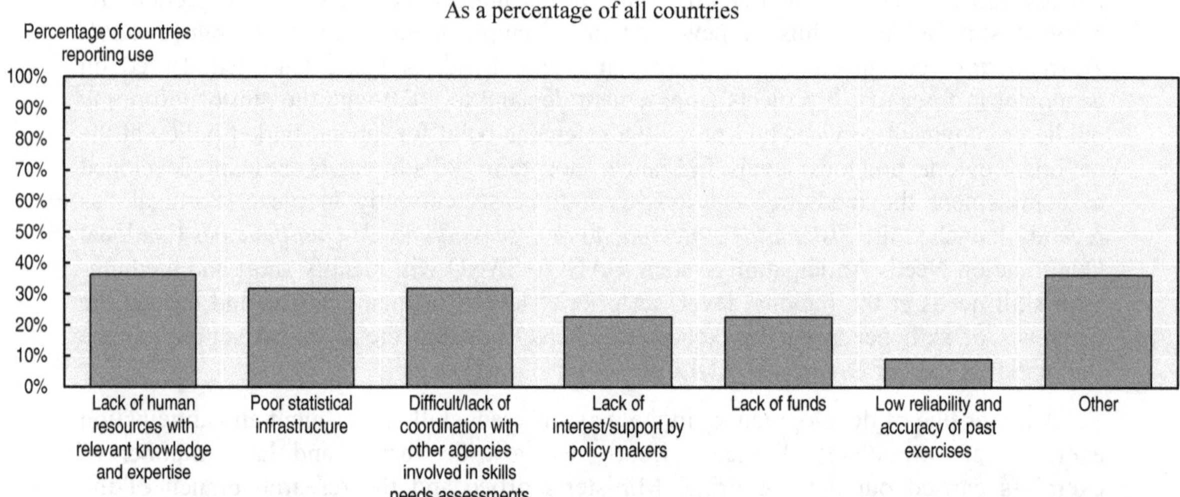

Note: Percentages based on responses from 22 countries with at least one obstacle identified (Austria, Belgium, Canada, Chile, the Czech Republic, Estonia, Finland, France, Germany, Greece, Hungary, Ireland, Italy, Korea, Norway, Portugal, the Slovak Republic, Slovenia, Spain, Sweden, Switzerland and Turkey). If more than one questionnaire was received per country, involvement is considered if reported in any questionnaire received.

Source: Questionnaire on Anticipating and Responding to Changing Skill Needs: Ministry of Labour and Ministry of Education questionnaires.

StatLink http://dx.doi.org/10.1787/888933333931

The economic crisis has further reduced the availability of resources to perform skills assessment and anticipation exercises in some countries, and this is likely to explain part of the concerns around the weak statistical infrastructures and lack of adequate human capital across the countries examined. In Slovenia, for instance, budget and staff cuts in the public sector are seen as one of the obstacles to developing future skills needs analyses. In Flanders (Belgium), further development, or even maintaining the regularity of existing exercises, is being threatened by the current cutbacks in public spending. Austria and Finland also report that the lack of funds puts a limit on the development of these exercises. The lack of funds is indirectly related to a lack of political will to support the development of such exercises (possibly because of the long-term investment that they require which exceeds the length of the typical political cycle) and to a potentially difficult collaboration between agencies.

Data availability is also mentioned as an obstacle to further development. It is particularly relevant in the context of scarce funds to develop the necessary instruments to collect the necessary data. In Flanders (Belgium), for example, there is sufficient information about the skill levels of those looking for work, vacancies available and employment by qualification levels, age and sector. There is, however, a dearth of data concerning the skill levels of people currently in work. In some instances, however, data availability is not simply a matter of funds, political will or co-ordination. In Norway and Canada, despite the intention to have better coverage at the regional level, the small population size of certain regions limits the capacity to assess and anticipate skill needs in these sparsely populated areas.

The past or perceived lack of reliability of exercises is not recognised as a major limitation to the development of skills assessment and anticipation exercises more generally. Long-term reliability has limited, however, the development of long-term forecasts in Lithuania and countries among the Baltic States (Martinaitis, 2012). Practically the most common obstacle to the development of skills assessment and anticipation exercises is "other", possibly highlighting the local challenges towards the development of these exercises.

Conclusions

At least one form of skills assessment or anticipation exercise is carried out in all countries. Exercises vary in the way they measure skills needs, frequently focusing on educational credentials or occupational demand as proxies. Only a minority of exercises assesses specific skills directly. Exercises also vary in the time span they consider; some focus on current skill needs, while others focus on short-term, medium-term or long-term skill needs. They also differ in the methods used to identify these skill needs. In line with best practice (see, CEDEFOP, 2008a; ETF, 2014), the majority of exercises draw their information from different sources, be they quantitative or qualitative. Few exercises, however, systematically mix qualitative and quantitative methods. In several countries there are efforts to better integrate quantitative and qualitative methods and as use qualitative data an important input to the exercises. Finally, exercises also vary in the way they cover the national, regional and sector levels, with the development of a comprehensive assessment or anticipation exercise covering all levels simultaneously in some countries, while in others there is a development of independent exercises for each type of analysis.

In most countries there are developments to current these exercises that increase their coverage, improve their methods or incorporate new exercises altogether. Although these developments can face obstacles like financing cutbacks, the fact that in a majority of countries there is movement towards the further development of these exercises is a testament to their perceived value and usefulness. In fact, skills assessment and anticipation exercises can be a valuable input to develop policies to reduce current or future skill shortages and mismatches. Most countries do use the information from these exercises to inform policy making, and this is discussed in further detail in Chapter 3 of this report.

Notes

1. General labour market information systems (LMI) monitor the labour market by periodically following, labour force participation, employment rates by sector and occupation, hours of work, wages and compensation costs and type of employment relationship, among other key statistics.

2. CEDEFOP (2008a) identifies Austria, France, Germany, the Netherlands, Sweden and the United Kingdom as countries with a holistic approach. At the time of their review, the Czech Republic, Estonia, Italy and Poland were building a holistic system.

References

Bartlett, W. (2012), "Skills Anticipation and Matching Systems in Transition and Developing Countries: Conditions and Challenges", European Training Foundation, Torino.

Castiglioni, G. and K. Tijdens (2014), "Skills and Occupational Needs: Labour Market Forecasting Systems in Italy", *Amsterdam Institute for Advanced Labour Studies Working Paper*, No. 142.

CEDEFOP (2012) "Building on Skills Forecasts – Comparing Methods and Applications, Conference Proceedings", *Research Paper*, No. 18.

CEDEFOP (2008a), "Systems for Anticipation of Skill Needs in the EU Member States", *CEDEFOP Working Paper*, No. 1.

CEDEFOP (2008b), *Future Skill Needs in Europe, Medium-Term Forecast: Synthesis Report*, European Office for Official Publications of the European Communities, Luxembourg.

Ciccarone, G. and Tancioni, M. (2012), "The FGB-LM Model: Structure and Recent Forecasts of the Italian Labour-Market Stock and Flows", *Building on Skills Forecasts – Comparing Methods and Applications, Conference Proceedings*, Research Paper, No. 18, CEDEFOP, pp. 147-168.

Colicchio, D. (2012), "EU Skills Anticipation Mapping Paper", European High Level Meeting on Skills Anticipation in Adult Learning, ESAAL, Torino, September 2012.

Commission of the European Communities (2009), "New Skills for New Jobs: Anticipating and Matching Labour Market and Skills Needs", COM(2008) 868 Final, Brussels.

DARES (2009), "La Nomenclature des Famille Professionnelles Version 2009, Table de Correspondance FAP/PCS/Rome", Ministère de l'Économie, de l'Industrie et de l'Emploi, Paris.

ETF (2014), *Foresight: Skills for the Future*, European Training Foundation, Torino.

Feiler, L. (2014), "Skills Needs Identification and Anticipation Policies and Practices in the Eastern Partnership Region: Cross-Country Report", Short Term High Quality Studies to Support Activities under the Eastern Partnership (HiQSTEP), EuropeAid/132574/C/SER/Multi.

Humpl, S. and D. Bacher (2012), "The AMS-Skills Barometer: A Web-Based Labour-Market Tool, Making Use of Forecast Results by Stakeholders", *Building on Skills Forecasts – Comparing Methods and Applications, Conference Proceedings*, Research Paper, No. 18, CEDEFOP, pp. 82-96.

Humpl, S. and M. Kargl (2008), "AMS-Skills Barometer – Austria's Target Group Oriented Labour Market Information System", in B. Kriechel and A. Schmid (eds.), *Regional Forecasting on Labour Markets*, Rainer Hampp Verlag, München, pp. 148-160.

ILO, OECD, World Bank Group (2014), *G20 Labour Markets: Outlook, Key Challenges and Policy Responses*, Report prepared for the G20 Labour and Employment Ministerial Meeting, Melbourne.

ISFOL (2014a), "Indagine Campionaria sulle Professioni" [Research on Occupations], ISFOL/ISTAT, Rome, available at: http://professionioccupazione.isfol.it//documenti/it/met_campionaria_2014.pdf (accessed 8 February, 2016).

ISFOL (2014b), "Indagine Audit sui Fabbisogni Professionali" [Audit on Occupational Needs Research], ISFOL/ISTAT, Rome, available at: http://professionioccupazione.isfol.it//documenti/it/met_%20audit_2014.pdf (accessed 8 February, 2016).

Lassnigg, L. (2012), *Anticipating and Matching Skills Demand and Supply: Synthesis of National Report*, European Training Foundation, Torino.

Mabotja, L. (2013), "Using the Delphi Method to Select Key Indicators for Skills Planning, Labour Market Intelligence Partnership", Pretoria.

Martinaitis, Ž. (2012), "Forecasting Skills Demand and Labour Market Dynamics in the Baltic States", *Building on Skills Forecasts – Comparing Methods and Applications, Conference Proceedings*, Research Paper, No. 18, CEDEFOP, pp. 97-110.

Migration Advisory Committee (2008), "Identifying Skilled Occupations where Migration Can Sensibly Help to Fill Labour Shortages: Methods of Investigation and Next Steps for the Committee's First Shortage Occupation List", Migration Advisory Committee, London.

Quintini, G. (2011), "Right for the Job: Over-Qualified or Under-Skilled?", *OECD Social, Employment and Migration Working Papers*, No. 120, OECD Publishing, Paris, http://dx.doi.org/10.1787/5kg59fcz3tkd-en.

Rasmussen, N. and P. Stephensen (2014), "A Microsimulation Model for Educational Forecasting", Conference Paper for the European Meeting of International Microsimulation Association, Maastricht, 23-24 October 2014.

Rosenthal, N. (1999), "Quality of BLS Projections: A Historical Account", *Monthly Labor Review*, Vol. 122, p. 27.

Shah, C. and G. Burke (2005), "Skills Shortages: Concepts, Measurement and Policy Responses", *Australian Bulletin of Labour*, Vol. 31, No. 1, p. 44.

UKCES (2010), *Skills for Jobs: Today and Tomorrow*, National Strategic Skills Audit for England 2010, Vol. : The Evidence Report, UK Commission for Employment and Skills, London.

Wilson, R. (2012), "Skills Forecasting: Applying the CEDEFOP Skills Forecasting Framework to Transition and Developing Countries", ETF Workshop on Foresight and Policies and Strategies for Vocational Education and Training (VET): Tools and Added Value in the Context of Transition and Developing Countries, Torino, March 2012.

Wilson, R. and A. Zukersteinova (2011), "Anticipating Changing Skill Needs: A Master Class," New Skills Network Event, Budapest, June 2011.

Wilson, R., I. Woolard and D. Le (2004), *Developing a National Skills Forecasting Tool for South Africa*, South African Department of Labour, Pretoria.

Youdi, V. and K. Hinchliffe (1985), *Forecasting Skilled Manpower Needs: The Experience of Eleven Countries*, International Institute for Educational Planning, UNESCO, Paris.

Chapter 3

Uses of skills assessment and anticipation exercises

In this chapter, a review is made of the policy uses that are made of the information produced by skills assessment and anticipation exercises. This highlights the wide spectrum of applications in the areas of employment, education and training, and migration policy. Moreover, the information is used not just by government ministries, but also by the social partners. That said, there are important barriers that hinder such information from being more fully or effectively exploited for policy purposes. Some of these relate to methodological issues inherent to the exercises themselves, while others are concerned with a lack of stakeholder involvement, the absence of consensus around skills needs, poor dissemination to a wider audience and the scattered nature of the policy response.

This chapter explores how governments and social partners use the information gathered from skills assessment and anticipation exercises to inform employment, education and migration policy. It also identifies the main barriers that prevent the information from these exercises to be used more extensively in policy making.

Main findings

- Information from skills assessment and anticipation exercises is used in all countries to inform policy or social partner action.
- In employment policy, they most commonly inform the development of occupational standards and worker training programmes.
- In education policy, they most commonly inform the design of educational programmes at the upper-secondary, tertiary or adult-education levels and the allocation of funding and student vacancies across these programmes.
- By identifying current or short-term future skill needs, they also inform migration policy by giving priorities to applicants with those skills.
- Two broad challenges are preventing skills assessment and anticipation exercises from being used more extensively to guide policy. First, the involvement and co-ordination of stakeholders need to be strengthened; and, second, there needs to be a good alignment between the design of the exercises and the expected policy uses.

The main uses of skills assessment and anticipation exercises

Skills-related policies involve many actors: ministries, education and training institutions, public employment services, employers, unions, workers and students and local/regional administrations, among others. This chapter shows that governments use information from skills assessment and anticipation exercises to update occupational standards; to design or revise training policies for workers or the unemployed; to design, revise or decide on the allocation of courses to provide in formal education, with this information being used in many countries to inform the development of VET programmes or apprenticeships. In addition, some governments use this information to guide migration policy as well as their transition to a digital or green economy. Social partners (employer organisations and trade unions) also use this information to lobby governments on education and employment policy, develop training programmes, or provide advice to their members on skill development. Both social partners and governments use this information for broad dissemination purposes to inform workers and students about trends in current or future skill demand and supply.

Informing employment policy

The information from skills assessment and anticipation exercises can feed into the development of employment and activation policies. It frequently informs the updating occupational standards or the development of on-the-job and re-training courses and systems (Figure 3.1).

Occupational standards

Skills assessment and anticipation exercises commonly inform the updating of occupational standards (Figure 3.1). Occupational standards identify the skills, qualifications and experience required to perform an occupation. They are then used to develop curricula and qualifications, for quality assurance or to guide the human development strategy of firms, among other uses. In the United Kingdom, for example, identified skill needs feed into the National Occupation Standards to fast track the development of standards in new occupations or occupations with changing skill requirements (UKCES, 2011). Updating occupational standards is identified as an important use of skills needs information in Australia, Chile, the Czech Republic, Finland, Japan, the Slovak Republic, Slovenia and Wallonia (Belgium). Chile, for example, uses regional-level labour market statistics to produce regional forecasts to define occupational profiles that determine entry requirements for the National Employment and Training Service's (*Servicio Nacional de Capacitación y Empleo*, SENCE) training offer. The Czech Republic involves employers through sector skills councils to consider their needs when updating occupational standards.

Figure 3.1. **The uses of skills assessment and anticipation exercises for employment policy**

As a percentage of all Ministry of Labour responses

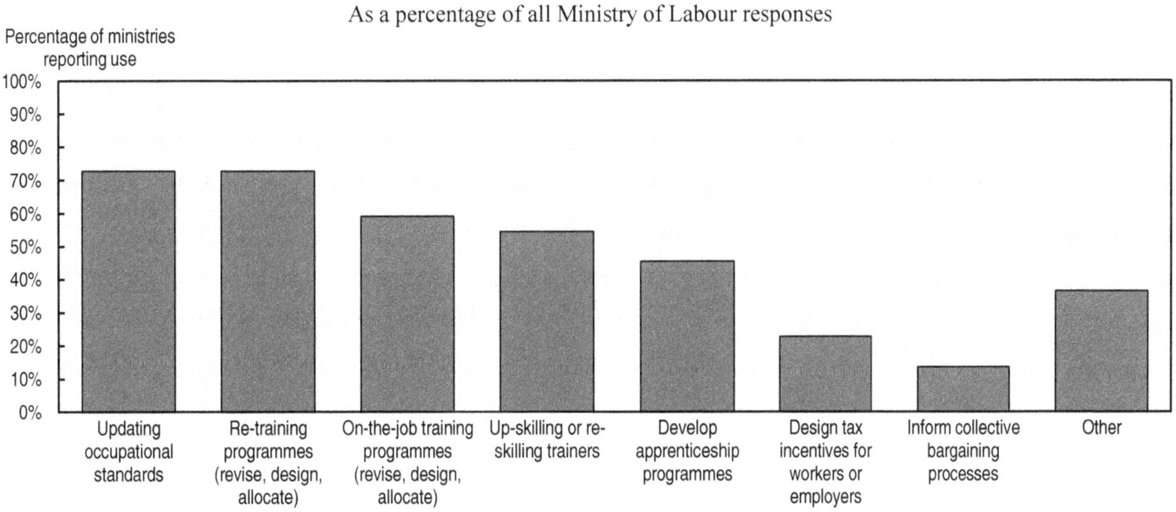

Percentage of ministries reporting use
100%
90%
80%
70%
60%
50%
40%
30%
20%
10%
0%
Updating occupational standards
Re-training programmes (revise, design, allocate)
On-the-job training programmes (revise, design, allocate)
Up-skilling or re-skilling trainers
Develop apprenticeship programmes
Design tax incentives for workers or employers
Inform collective bargaining processes
Other

Note: Percentages based on 21 countries with at least one employment policy use reported (Australia, Austria, Belgium, Canada, Chile, the Czech Republic, Denmark, Estonia, Finland, France, Germany, Japan, Korea, the Netherlands, Norway, Poland, Portugal, the Slovak Republic, Slovenia, Switzerland and the United States).

Source: Questionnaire on Anticipating and Responding to Changing Skill Needs: Ministry of Labour Questionnaire.

StatLink http://dx.doi.org/10.1787/888933333982

Re-training, on-the-job training and apprenticeship programmes

Another common use of skills assessment and anticipation exercises is to inform re-training, on-the-job training programmes and/or apprenticeship schemes. This is an important use in Australia, Austria, Belgium (Flanders and Wallonia) the Czech Republic, Denmark, France, Japan and Portugal. Japan's offer of vocational training for workers who plan to change their job or improve their skills is based on local labour market and industrial needs. Analyses of skills assessments and forecasts carried out by the public employment service and the regional branches of the Ministry of Labour, Health and Welfare inform the provision of these programmes. Skills assessment and anticipation exercises also inform the design of new Japanese on-the-job training programmes. In France, one of the main purposes for doing skills assessments, forecast and foresight exercises is to guide education and training programmes, particularly on-the-job training programmes. Public employment services in Belgium (both Flanders and Wallonia) also actively guide the training of the unemployed towards occupations identified in shortage. In Wallonia (Belgium), for example, information on skills shortages and mismatches informs the provision of specific training programmes and sessions, as well as skill validation programmes. In Turkey, the public employment service is one of the organisations that lead skills assessment and anticipation exercises and uses them to inform re-training programmes and active labour market programmes.

Austria's public employment service (*Arbeitsmarktservice*, AMS) monitors the labour market outcomes and trends of 24 vocational fields through the Qualification Barometer. AMS also has a "Standing Committee on New Skills" through which, in collaboration with social partners, specialist groups identify short- to medium-term skills needs in professional areas to guide both on-the-job training and re-training programmes. In Estonia, the allocation of training opportunities and the definition of priority areas for training for the unemployed take into account future skills needs and future strategic development priorities. These priority areas are revised twice a year to ensure flexibility and reactivity of these active labour market programmes.

In response to the current shortages in the IT sector, the White House has launched TechHire. It is a USD 100 million programme that provides training through universities, community colleges and "coding camps" to equip workers with coding skills. It is based on the fact that a four-year university degree in computer science is not always required for many of the IT jobs in offer even though many employers seek credentialed computer scientists. Training programmes are coupled with outreach with employers to guide them to recognise coding skills in jobseekers that have not completed a four-year computer science degree. To this end, TechHire has developed a standardised assessment to gauge candidates' coding skills.

Skills assessment and anticipation exercises also inform the development of apprenticeship programmes. Germany's Federal Institute for Vocational Education and Training (BIBB) carries out short-term econometric models to forecast the supply and demand for apprenticeship places for the following year. One of the direct uses of skill needs assessments in Australia, Northern Ireland and Turkey is to promote apprenticeships in occupations and industries with greater demand for skilled labour. Australia does this by directing the funds allocated to training organisations (see Box 3.1) and Northern Ireland by extending the funds available for apprenticeships in these sectors to candidates of all ages, not just youth. Turkey gives priority to work-based learning programmes in occupations in need, as determined by the Provincial Employment and Vocational Training Boards following analyses of the annual Labour Market Surveys (OECD, 2014a).

Other employment policy uses

By contrast, the information from skills assessment and anticipation exercises is rarely used to inform collective bargaining processes, for staff planning in public companies, or to devise incentives for employers or workers. The exceptions are France, Finland, New Zealand and Wallonia (Belgium) (where skills assessment and anticipation exercises feed into collective bargaining processes) and Australia, Canada, Flanders (Belgium), the Netherlands, New Zealand and Wallonia (Belgium) (where such information is used to generate economic incentives for the hiring of workers with specific skills or for employers to up-skill or re-skill workers in specific sectors). The Canada Job Grant is an employer driven approach that supports workers and unemployed individuals to gain the skills and training they need to help fill available jobs. Employers or organisations acting on behalf of employers, may apply for government funding of up to CAD 10 000 per person, towards the direct cost of training. Employers are required to contribute on average an additional 1/3 to these costs. Also, Canada's Targeted Initiative for Older Workers (TIOW) was recently renewed and had its eligibility criteria broadened so that, in addition to communities with high unemployment and/or significant downsizing/closures, communities with unmet demand and/or skills mismatches can now participate. Following the 2010 Canterbury earthquake, New Zealand has provided financial incentives (e.g. relocation assistance) for the unemployed to relocate to Canterbury to work in occupations in need (OECD, 2015).

Informing education policy

The results from skills assessment and anticipation exercises also feed into education policy. In most countries, information from skill assessment and anticipation exercises is used to design new qualifications, revise curricula or decide what courses to fund or provide at the adult training, upper-secondary or tertiary levels. They are also commonly used to update qualifications frameworks, as is the case in Portugal. Portugal's SANQ is used to adapt education and training pathways in updating the National Qualifications Catalogue (Figure 3.2).

Determining student numbers and course contents

In several countries skills needs assessments or skills forecast and foresight exercises are used to determine student numbers, vacancies offered by fields of study, or course contents in the provision of formal education and training. In Norway, for example, the expected lack of engineers, teachers and health professionals was an important input to decide the educational offer of post-secondary education vacancies. The low number of graduates from STEM fields and their low skill levels has promoted a specific lifelong skills development strategy in STEM fields in 2006-10 that was renewed in 2010 and in 2014 (Norwegian Ministry for Education and Research, 2006, 2010). In Germany, the BIBB-IAB Qualification and Occupational Fields forecasts highlighted the increased demand for workers with medium-level skills and the corresponding need to develop this labour supply. In New Zealand, the expected shortage of STEM-related skills and other highly skilled professions led to the increase in university vacancies and reduced tuition feeds for related programmes (OECD, 2015). In the Netherlands, the expected shortage of STEM-related skills motivated the *Techniekpact* in 2013 whereby several ministries work together with social partners and regional authorities to increase the number of students enrolled in STEM fields and strengthen the links between the education system and labour market needs.

Austria, Estonia, Germany, Italy, Portugal and Sweden all use skills assessment and anticipation exercises in different ways to determine the provision of post-secondary education; the same is true for Denmark, Finland and Ireland (Commission of the European Communities, 2009). In order to receive accreditation for new programmes, Austrian legislation requires that Universities of Applied Sciences (*Fachhochschulen*) complete a Demand and Acceptance survey that evaluates the projected demand for each qualification seeking accreditation. Skills assessments are also integrated in the curriculum development process in Austrian universities. Germany's Standing Conference of the Ministers of Education and Cultural Affairs of the *Länder* (KMK) develops educational planning using forecasts of future school pupils and university applicants. Portugal, through the National Agency for Qualifications and Vocational Education and Training (ANQEP), carries out anticipation exercises with the explicit purpose of guiding VET development and prioritise fields of study, as do Italy's new *Instituti Tecnici Superiori* (ITS, Higher Technical Institutes). Swedish higher education institutions, through reports produced by the Swedish National Agency for Higher Education (*Högskoleverket*), use forecasts produced by Statistics Sweden to plan the number of vacancies to available in their programmes. Although Swedish higher education institutions are autonomous in deciding their vacancies, the Swedish Government has made some adjustments in vacancies for certain professions in response to current and expected imbalances (e.g. health care and engineering). The Swedish Agency for Higher Vocational Education (*Myndigheten för Yrkeshögskolan*) also determines whether a profession or qualification is in demand by employers and industries, so that VET development follows employer and industry demand. In Finland, employment forecasts are translated into education needs in the National Education Development Plan, and subsequently used to determine the offer of vacancies by field and sector (Department for Education and Science Policy, 2012). In Estonia, decisions on VET and adult education training volumes take into account forecasted skills needs, employment outcomes of graduates from different VET programmes, as well as input from a number of other ministries (e.g. Ministries of Social Affairs, Agriculture or Economic Affairs) and social partners. Vacancies in Estonia's higher education system followed a similar mechanism. However, since the 2013 reforms of the higher education system, vacancies have been determined by each institution individually. Labour demand forecasts do remain a source of information in the regulation of higher education, however, with the predicted need for specialists with higher education in the labour market being one of the elements used to allocate public funds to universities.

Information for students, families and workers

In many countries, skills assessment and anticipation exercises feed into information systems for students, families and workers about the labour market prospects of different occupations. Finland, for example, has recently launched a web-based system, ForeOccupation (*ForeAmmatti*, available in Finnish at www.foreammatti.fi (accessed 8 February, 2016), to be used by students and workers. It provides information on vacancies, regional supply and demand of labour, skills needed in the workplace and the level of competition for jobs, now and in the future. Students and workers can input a particular occupation (e.g. pharmacist) and region (e.g. Pohjois-Karjala), and the system will return the average number of job openings in the region per month based on both historical and projected data (e.g. one vacancy per month), the regions where those occupations are in greatest demand and the degree to which competition for jobs in these occupations will change in the forthcoming years. The information is based on data from public employment services, analysis of job announcements and forecasts. *ForeAmmatti* is also oriented towards experts in the public employment service, as they can get detailed information for the purposes of policy planning and programme design.

Although in many countries information is provided to students and workers about labour market prospects, it is perhaps surprising that information from skills assessment and anticipation exercises is rarely used to update career guidance. Finland's *ForeAmmati*, inasmuch it feeds into counselling is an exception; as is Germany. So is Norway that is developing and improving its career guidance system following OECD recommendations (OECD, 2014b); and Portugal which has created a network of 242 Centres for Qualification and Vocational Education to guide young people and adults through the qualifying pathways of the National Qualifications Catalogue (Figure 3.2).

Figure 3.2. **The use of skills assessment and anticipation exercises for education policy**

As a percentage of all Ministry of Education responses

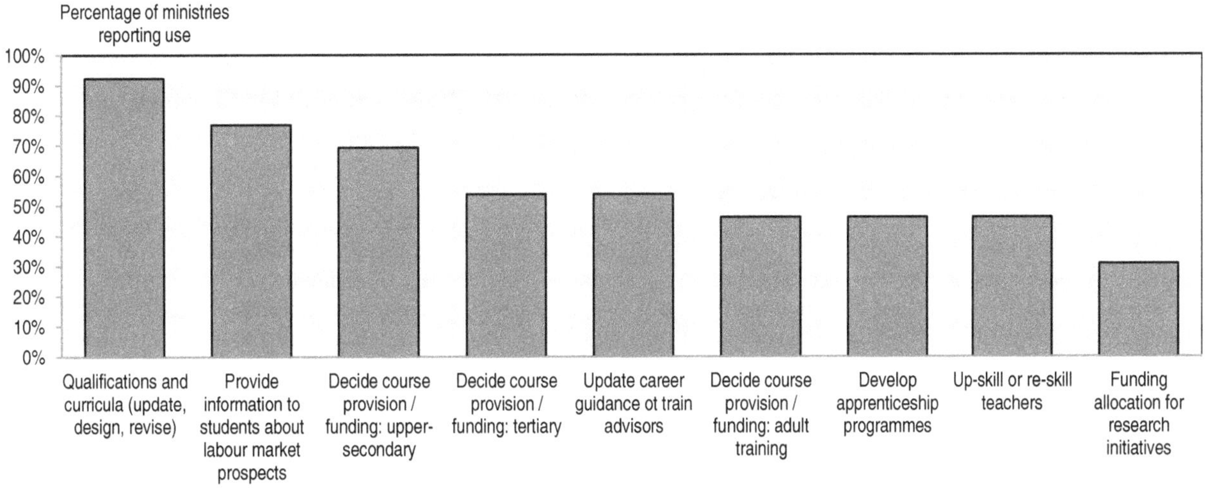

Note: Percentages based on 13 countries with at least one education policy use reported (Austria, Belgium, Chile, Finland, Germany, Hungary, Ireland, Italy, Norway, Portugal, Spain, Sweden and Turkey).

Source: Questionnaire on Anticipating and Responding to Changing Skill Needs: Ministry of Education Questionnaire.

StatLink http://dx.doi.org/10.1787/888933333994

Informing migration and other policy

Immigration policy

In some countries like Australia, Belgium, Canada, Denmark, Ireland, France, New Zealand, Sweden and the United Kingdom, the agencies in charge of migration draw on information from skills assessment and anticipation exercises to inform migration policy (Chaloff and Lemaitre, 2009; OECD, 2014c; Ruhs and Anderson, 2010). Of course, this is only possible in the context of countries that have the possibility of modifying their migration policy accordingly. In Australia, Belgium and New Zealand, skills assessment and anticipation information produced by the Ministries in charge of Labour and Industry are used to place occupations in high demand on special shortage lists (e.g. the Skilled Occupations List (SOL) in Australia, the Skill Shortage List (SSL) in New Zealand or the Labour Shortage List in Sweden). Workers with skills required in those occupations do not have to be sponsored by an employer when applying for a permanent visa (see Box 3.1). For semi-skilled and unskilled occupations not included in New Zealand's shortage list, the Canterbury Skills Hub first matches national jobseekers with employer vacancies; if no national jobseeker is identified, the Hub provides a letter to support fast tracked visa applications (OECD, 2015). The Canadian Occupational Projection System (COPS) projects the number of jobseekers coming from the school system and from migration in conjunction with projected labour demand. COPS identifies occupations that have been either facing current shortages recently or that are likely to face future employment pressures.[1] This information was used by the agency in charge of immigration to define priority occupations for the Federal Skilled Worker Programme.[2] The Centre for Canadian Language Benchmarks also draws on current skills assessment of migrant workers to describe, measure and recognise the English or French language skills of immigrants and to improve their integration into the Canadian labour market.

Information from skills forecasts is used to select occupations and trades targeted for action under the Pan-Canadian Framework for the Recognition of Foreign Qualifications – a programme that seeks to ease the integration of workers with foreign qualifications through the adequate recognition of credentials earned abroad.

Box 3.1. **The Australian Skilled Occupations List and the New Zealand Skill Shortage List**

For over three decades, the Australian Department of Employment identifies current skill shortages on a regular and systematic basis to construct a Skilled Occupations List (SOL). It draws on the Survey of Employers who has Recently Advertised (SERA) to identify pressures in occupations that require a longer training time. Through discussions with employers and recruitment professionals, as well as through quantitative analysis of recently advertised vacancies, occupations are classified as "in shortage", "in recruitment difficulty" or "no shortage" at the national, state/territory and metropolitan area levels. Occupations in difficulty are characterised based on whether employers' difficulty in filling the vacancies is due to a lack of applicants, or a lack of skills or a lack of experience among the pool of applicants (Department of Employment, 2014a).

The August 2014 update to the SOL 2013-14 added 30 occupations to the list (which currently has 191 occupations). As an example, automotive electricians were added to the list because employers in states other than Tasmania, Northern Territory and Western Australia had difficulty attracting suitable applicants. Only a small proportion of applicants are considered to be suitable." (Department of Employment, 2014, p. 2). Chefs were included in the SOL because "employers attract multiple applicants but many are considered to be unsuitable as they lack the required level of experience or skill in a particular cuisine or establishment type. Employers are ideally seeking apprenticeship-qualified chefs/cooks. Positions for senior or highly experienced chefs are particularly difficult to fill" (Department of Employment, 2014b, p. 4)

New Zealand develops both an immediate and long term Skill Shortage Lists (ISSL and LTSSL). Industry stakeholders (e.g. employer groups, trade unions, industry training bodies) submit proposals for occupations to be included in the list. The evidence to support the inclusion/removal of occupations from the list is then reviewed. The lists are updated twice a year with details on specific skill requirements for specific occupations (Immigration New Zealand, 2014a, p. 17). As an example, as of the second semester of 2014, the LTSSL included a "Statistician (Fisheries Modeller) with skill requirements of a Masters or PhD degree in science, statistics, mathematics, statistical modelling or another relevant discipline and a minimum of one year's relevant post-qualification work experience" or an "Electrician with certification equivalent to full or limited certification from New Zealand's Electrical Workers Registration Board (bonus points are awarded for applicants with registration from New Zealand's Electrical Workers Registration Board)" (Immigration New Zealand, 2014b, p. 18).

Australia's SOL and New Zealand's ISSL/LTSSL are publicly available and widely used. They are considered in a range of employment, education and training and migration policies. In Australia, for example, priority in the funding for training organisations is given to programmes in the SOL (OECD, 2014a). In the case of migration, both the SOL and ISSL/LTSSL information is used to decide which workers can apply for permanent residency without having to be sponsored by an employer or family member, or be nominated by a state or territory government (e.g. Australia's Independent Skilled Migration programme, New Zealand's Essential Skills work visas). Australian agencies validate workers' skills and workers are awarded points for age, English language ability, overseas employment, educational qualifications, partner skills and other areas. Eligibility is determined if migrant workers satisfy a minimum cut-off of points.

Source: Department of Employment (2014), *Skill Shortage Research Methodology*, Australian Government, Canberra; Department of Employment (2014), *Skill Shortage List Australia 2013-14*, Australian Government, Canberra; Immigration New Zealand (2014), *Reviewing the Essential Skills in Demand Lists*, Ministry of Business, Innovation and Employment, Wellington; Immigration New Zealand (2014), *Long Term Skill Shortage List – June 2014*, Ministry of Business, Innovation and Employment, Wellington. OECD (2014), "Background Paper Prepared by the OECD", *G20, OECD, EC Conference on Quality Apprenticeships for Giving Youth a Better Start in the Labour Market*, OECD Conference Centre, Paris, 9 April 2014.

Promoting green growth and the transition to the digital economy

Green growth will see new sectors and activities develop and, in some cases, displace other activities with the possibility of skills imbalance emerging (OECD, 2011). Similarly, the transition to a digital economy will change the skill needs in occupations directly related to the ICT sector as well as those unrelated to the ICT sector. Skills assessment and anticipation exercises can play a role in facilitating these transitions by reducing job displacement and ensuring the skills needed in these transitions are available in the labour market. However, only Austria, Belgium (Flanders and Wallonia) France, Germany, Greece, Hungary, Ireland, Italy and Turkey explicitly relate the results of skills assessment and anticipation exercises to the transition to a greener economy. Only in Austria, Belgium (Flanders and Wallonia), Canada, Denmark, France, Hungary, Ireland, Italy, Norway, Portugal and Turkey exercises consider the transition to the digital economy. In all these cases, skills assessment and anticipation exercises usually provide information regarding skill needs in these transitions; they are less frequently used to inform specific policies and programmes. *Ad-hoc* and sector-specific analyses have been carried out in Greece to determine the skill content for professions in the environmental and digital sectors. Germany has recently commissioned a foresight exercise to explore the impact of digitalisation on the labour market's skill needs.

In Canada and France, information from skills assessment and anticipation exercises is used in policies related to the transition to the digital economy and in policies specific to the ICT sector. Occupations related to the digital economy are included in the Canadian Occupational Projection System (COPS) and in the assessment of recent occupational labour market conditions. In addition, the Sectoral Initiatives Programme (SIP) funds ongoing monitoring of the labour market and key economic drivers that have an impact on the ICT sector's productivity (e.g. five-year forecasts, measures of job readiness and career paths in STEM education programmes). SIP will also support the update the National Occupational Standards (NOS) and accreditation regime for jobseekers and employers in the ICT sector. In addition, the Department of Employment and Social Development Canada (ESDC) has asked the Council of Canadian Academies to study how well Canada is prepared to meet future skill requirements in STEM fields. ESDC has also linked information from ICT sectors to feed into the Temporary Foreign Workers Programme.

In Ireland, in 2010, the Expert Group on Future Skills Needs carried out a study on the skills needed for firms working in the "Green Economy sector" and another study on digital skill needs. The assessment of future skill requirements in the green economy anticipates, for example, that job opportunities will arise within domestic and export markets, both through the growth of the green sector and through employment opportunities that arise outside the green sector as firms transition to the adoption of green processes (Expert Group on Future Skills Needs, 2010). Specific exercises specifically related to the digital economy have also been commissioned, as has the assessment of future skill needs requirement of the digital media industry (Expert Group on Future Skills Needs, 2006). Information from these studies has fed into Ireland's Action Plan for Jobs (Government of Ireland, 2012, 2013).

In line with the national strategy and national pact to transition towards a green economy, France has established the National observatory for green economy jobs and skills (*Observatoire national des emplois et métiers de l'économie verte*). The observatory follows green growth and monitors the sectoral and macroeconomic impact of this transition, with special attention to its implications for jobs and skills

(Commissariat Général au Développement Durable, 2014). A The forecasts and a national strategic orientation to a Green Economy have created partnerships with social partners like the trade unions, employer organisations and the public employment service. The public employment service (*Pôle Emploi*), for example, has studied the supply and demand for green skills to create programmes to up- or re-skill jobseekers to better meet the requirements of this transition (Pôle Emploi, 2011a, 2011b).

In Italy, the provision of VET programmes at the post-secondary level follows an analysis of local needs in the context of the implementation of policies regarding environmental and social sustainability in the productive and building sectors. Programmes are thus designed to provide students with skills such as: the ability to evaluate the environmental impact of energy systems, the ability to select and apply innovative technologies, the ability to enforce regulations on safety and environmental quality, the ability to intervene in the management of waste water, waste and emissions and the ability to apply methodology for environmental and strategic impact assessments.

In Austria and Norway, specific studies on the skill needs brought by these transitions have been carried out – though the policy implications have not necessarily translated into specific policies. Such exercises are being planned in Germany. Austria's public employment service's (*Arbeitsmarktservice Österreich*, AMS) Standing Committee on New Skills has the objective of anticipating the qualifications required in the medium term and take measures accordingly. Following the results of working groups, the Committee has concluded that, in addition to processes of tertiarisation and the greater demand for both general and special skills, ecologisation (i.e. growth in green jobs) and technologisation (i.e. growth of the digital economy) will pose challenges to firms and jobseekers (Bliem et al., 2011). Norway has also commissioned a study to forecast future supply and demand for advanced ICT competences up to 2030. It recommends the establishment of a regular monitoring system of supply and demand of advanced ICT skills. Results and recommendations of the Norwegian assessment are recent, and in the coming months, the Ministries of Education, Local Government and Modernisation and Trade, Industry and Fisheries will convene to discuss the recommendations (DAMVAD, 2014).

The use by social partners

In addition to governments, social partners are key users of information from skills assessment and anticipation exercises. For both trade union confederations and employer organisations, the most common use of this information is to lobby education or employment policy (Figure 3.3). They also use this information to advise their members on skills to promote within their firms or among their workers, and to provide information for a wider audience. Trade unions are, in contrast to governments and employer organisations, likely to use information from assessment and anticipation exercises to inform collective bargaining processes.

Figure 3.3. **The use of skills assessment and anticipation exercises by social partners**

As a percentage of all trade union and employer organisation responses

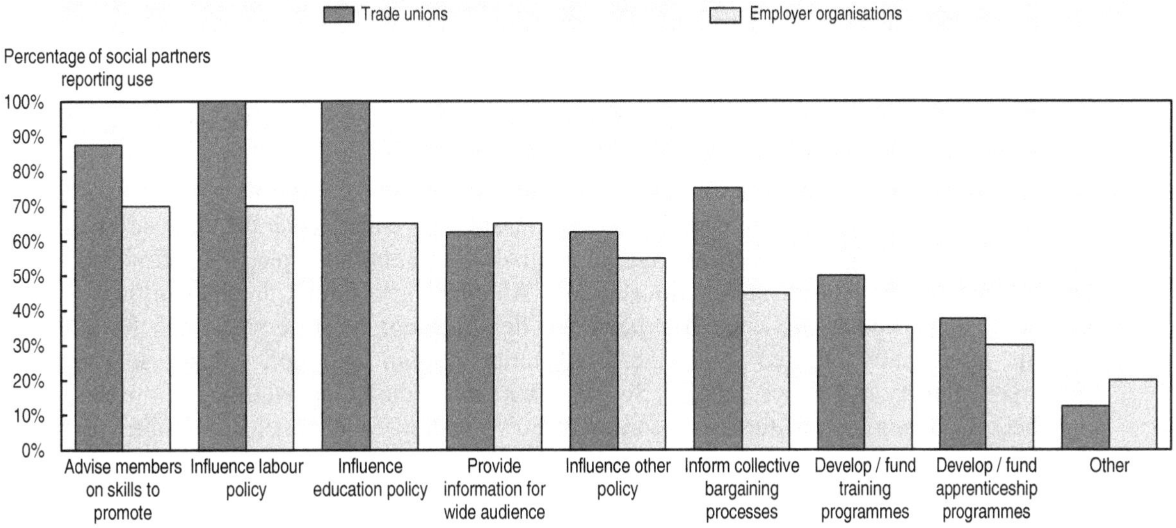

Note: Percentages based on responses from 20 employer organisations with at least one use reported (Canada (2 employer organisation responses), Chile, the Czech Republic, Denmark (2), Finland, France, Germany, Greece, Ireland, Japan (2), Korea, the Netherlands, Norway, Portugal, Spain, the Slovak Republic and Slovenia) and eight trade union confederations with at least one use reported (Denmark, Finland, France, Norway, Spain (2 trade union responses), Sweden and the United Kingdom).

Source: Questionnaire on Anticipating and Responding to Changing Skill Needs: Employers' Organisation and Trade Union questionnaires.

StatLink http://dx.doi.org/10.1787/888933334001

Disseminating results to a wider audience

The results from skills assessment and anticipation exercises are generally relevant to a broad audience: policy makers, stakeholders, social partners, sectoral organisations, practitioners and individuals. The challenge for many exercises is to capitalise on this potential interest while considering the complex methodology and that these tools are not manpower planning techniques (Humpl and Bacher, 2012). In general, both ministries and social partners share the results from skills assessment and anticipation exercises with a broader public. They do so primarily by developing reports and websites. A majority ministries and social partners take advantage of public media (TV, radio, newspapers or magazines) to disseminate findings and analysis. They rarely rely on social media to disseminate such information. The Netherlands is the only country that uses social media to disseminate the findings from their skills assessment and anticipation exercises. Only in two countries are no attempts made at wider dissemination: in Chile (where exercises are carried out by private employer organisations or have a specific regional focus to inform training) and in Portugal (where the exercises feed into very specific training policies and public employment service programmes).

While both ministries and social partners generally attempt to disseminate information on skills needs more widely, they also recognise that more can be done in this respect (Table 3.1). As discussed below, there is a need for the developers of skills anticipation exercises to engage their audience more effectively. One way to do this is to recognise that the "wider audience" is a constellation of users, each valuing the information from skills assessment and anticipation exercises differently and each expecting it to serve different uses. In this respect some agencies present the information from these exercises in different ways, depending on the audience. The Austrian public employment service's Qualification Barometer has two interfaces. One for jobseekers focuses on job vacancies and training opportunities. The other, for experts and other users, focuses on labour-market developments and information on occupations and skills (Humpl and Bacher, 2012). Canada's Department of Employment and Social Development highlights that centralising the dissemination of labour market information and skills assessment on a single platform (Job Bank) has been a successful initiative. Job Bank provides an interactive experience for users, tailoring the information to users' interests. Additionally, through a modernised Job Bank, the enhanced Job Match service of Job Bank for Employers will strengthen the role that Job Bank plays in providing detailed and timely labour market information. Another successful Canadian initiative tailored to a particular audience has been the development of a seminar, the Skills Summit, specifically tailored to business, education, labour and policy leaders. The Slovenian Ministry of Labour, Family, Social Affairs and Equal Opportunities comments that the best dissemination tools are conferences, workshops and panel discussions. In Sweden, a special effort is being made to raise awareness on the availability of information, while in Norway, researchers from Statistics Norway are available for contact with the press and are able to explain the findings in a simple way.

Barriers to the use of skills assessment and anticipation exercises in policy making

Ministries of Labour and Education, employer organisations and trade union confederations were asked about the barriers that prevented information from skills assessment and anticipation exercises from being effectively translated into policy. Respondents identified and ranked the importance of 19 barriers relating to either methodological, dissemination or policy development aspects of the process.

In general, the barriers identified speak to two broad challenges: the first is how to involve and co-ordinate stakeholders; the second is how to bring the skills assessment and anticipation exercises closer to the needs and requirements of policy makers.

Table 3.1 shows that eight of the ten most common responses identified by ministries are also identified by social partners, although they are often ranked differently.[3] For governments, a common concern that limits the policy use of skills assessment and anticipation exercises is that the resulting information does not meet the requirements of policy makers. Results are not sufficiently disaggregated: national-level results may not be useful to make decisions at a local level, or broad occupational categories may not provide the evidence to make decisions about specific training provision. Similarly, the way skills are measured and defined in the exercises do not easily map to useful variables in the policy-making sphere. For example, for education and training providers information about trends for specific occupations may not translate directly into the specific skills and courses/fields-of-study to be promoted. In addition, labour supply/demand dynamics are often not sufficiently considered to give an adequate picture of present and future skill needs. An example of this last point is the United States, where there are currently good occupational forecasts that can are translated to skill needs using occupational surveys like O*NET, but forecasts give insufficient consideration to components of the skill supply (e.g. migration projections or projections of graduation by fields of study).

The barriers identified by social partners overlap somewhat with those highlighted by ministries, but there are some notable differences. Specific stakeholders may have different priorities and interests and a different perceived role in skills assessment and anticipation exercises. While almost two-thirds of ministries report that results are not sufficiently disaggregated as a barrier, this is the case for half of the social partners. Three of the four most common barriers identified by ministries refer to the alignment of the exercise to policy making, yet none of these barriers feature among the four most common reported by the social partners (possibly because their role is more about influencing, rather than making, policy). Ministries also report stakeholder involvement as a barrier, but in their opinion, the barrier is more about making the results available than effectively engaging with other stakeholders in the decisional/policy process; the lack of consultation with stakeholders in identifying skill needs is considered a barrier by only 30% of ministries but by 75% of social partners. Reaching consensus is considered a barrier by 63% of social partners but this barrier does not feature among the ten most common identified by ministries (it is identified by only 22% of ministries). Another common barriers for ministries include how sharing results with a wider audience in a way that is not too technical (even though practically all disseminate the information in one way or another).

Social partners report that many of the most important barriers relate to stakeholder's involvement in identifying skill needs and in the ensuing dialogue. Social partners feel that key stakeholders should have a more prominent role in identifying skill needs, in discussing results and in ensuring that consensus is reached before developing or implementing policies. Carrying out foresight exercises, giving skills councils a prominent role in skills assessment and anticipation exercises (as done in Australia, Finland and the United Kingdom, for example) and the involvement of social partners in the Expert Group for Future Skills Needs in Ireland can be mechanisms to overcome this barrier (Chapter 4 develops the mechanisms in place to facilitate the effective involvement of stakeholders).

Many countries report that the sparse nature of a skills policy response (across different government agencies and/or regional/sub-regional administrative levels) is a barrier to the effective policy use of skills assessment and anticipation information. This points to an important co-ordination challenge when it comes to skills policies and that could be eased with a national skills strategy (e.g. Ireland, Portugal) or inter-ministerial skills working groups (e.g. the United States). Finally, several ministries report that the lack of flexibility of governments to impact education or labour market policy is also a barrier.

In all, these barriers speak to the governance of skills assessment and anticipation exercises. They speak to the forms, challenges and mechanisms of stakeholder involvement and how the design of the exercises can be brought closer to policy making. Multiple stakeholders are involved in all countries (different government agencies, regional/sub-regional administrative levels and social partners) – albeit with different degrees of success. Involvement takes place whether in the development of the skills assessment and anticipation exercises, in the discussion of the results or in the development of a policy response. Disagreements about skills needs and the corresponding policy response can arise in this process, but mechanisms to overcome such disagreements and successfully involve and co-ordinate stakeholders in the process do exist, and will also be discussed further in Chapter 4.

Table 3.1. **Ten most common barriers limiting the translation of skills assessment and anticipation information to effective policies**

As a percentage of all Ministries of Labour/Education and Trade Unions/Employer organisations

Ministries of Labour / Education		Trade Union Confederations/Employer Organisations	
Barrier	%	Barrier	%
Results are not sufficiently disaggregated	63	**Lack of consultation with stakeholders on identifying skill needs**	75
Results are not sufficiently shared with a wider audience	56	**Policy response is scattered across government levels or agencies**	67
Output is too technical	52	**Results are not sufficiently discussed with key stakeholders**	63
The way skills are measured and defined do not map to useful variables in policy-making	48	No consensus on skills needs is reached	63
Lack of consideration of key labour supply/demand dynamics	48	**Lack of consideration of key labour supply/demand dynamics**	54
Policy response is scattered across government levels or agencies	48	**Results are not sufficiently shared with key stakeholders**	54
Results are not sufficiently shared with key stakeholders	41	**Results are not sufficiently disaggregated**	50
Results are not sufficiently discussed with key stakeholders	37	Time inconsistencies between the production of information and planning/policy cycles	46
Local governments lack the flexibility or tools to impact education or labour market policy	33	**Results are not sufficiently shared with a wider audience**	46
Lack of consultation with stakeholders on identifying skill needs	30	**The way skills are measured and defined do not map to useful variables in policy-making**	38

Note: Ministries of Labour/Education take into account the 27 responses from either ministry reporting at least one barrier [Austria (2 responses), Belgium (3), Canada, Chile (2), Denmark, Estonia, Finland, France, Germany (2), Hungary, Ireland, Korea, the Netherlands, Norway (2), Poland, Portugal, Slovenia, Spain, Switzerland, Turkey and the United States]. Trade unions and employer organisations consider the 26 responses from either social partner with at least one barrier identified [Canada (2 responses), Chile, Denmark (3), Finland (2), France, Germany, Greece, Ireland, Japan (2), Korea, the Netherlands, Norway (2), Portugal, the Slovak Republic, Slovenia, Spain (2), Sweden (2) and the United Kingdom]. The ten most common barriers identified by ministries or social partners are shown. In bold the barriers that are among the ten most common for both ministries and social partners. A total of 19 barriers were proposed in the questionnaire. In the case of ties in the percentage of barriers identified, those with the higher average importance are ranked higher.

Source: Questionnaire on Anticipating and Responding to Changing Skill Needs: Ministry of Labour, Ministry of Education, Employer Organisation and Trade Union questionnaires.

StatLink http://dx.doi.org/10.1787/888933334018

Conclusions

Skills assessment and anticipation exercises can potentially inform education and labour policy as well as other areas of public policy. They are used across countries: to inform the number of vacancies in VET or higher education, to inform the design and allocation of on-the-job or re-training programmes, to design and revise occupational standards, or to inform apprenticeship programmes, among other common uses. They are also used to inform the development of migration policy, giving priority to applicants with skills suitable for occupations in current or expected shortage. In some countries the information from skills assessment and anticipation exercises is used to inform the economy's transition to a green and/or digital economy.

Governments are but one of the potential users of the information from skills assessment and anticipation exercises. Trade union confederations and employer organisations use this information to influence government policy, to advise their members and to inform both collective bargaining processes and spur wide dissemination.

Although information from skills assessment and anticipation exercises is used in all countries to inform public policy and stakeholder activity, governments and stakeholders all recognise the existence of barriers that hinder further use of this information in policy making. Barriers frequently include the level and quality of involvement of stakeholders or a wider audience in: the development of the exercises; the discussion of the results; and/or the development of the corresponding policy response. The tools to ensure that this involvement and collaboration is effective is analysed in the next chapter.

Notes

1. The Canadian Occupational Projection System's assessment of recent occupational labour market conditions (or recent skill pressures) is often viewed as equivalent to "current" conditions, although current conditions may differ from recent ones

2. As of 2015, the Federal Skilled Worker Programme was replaced by the so-called Expression of Interest programme; it is unclear how the Expression of Interest Programme will use information from skills assessment and anticipation exercises.

3. There is no complete country overlap between the ministry and social partner responses in terms of their countries. Thus, differences in the barriers identified between ministries and social partners may reflect the different country contexts rather than their opinion with skills assessment and anticipation exercises more broadly.

References

Bliem, W., S. Weiss and G. Grün (2011), "AMS Standing Committee on New Skills 2010/2011: Report on the Results of the Expert Groups", *AMS Info*, Vol. 211.

Chaloff, J. and G. Lemaitre (2009), "Managing Highly-Skilled Labour Migration: A Comparative Analysis of Migration Policies and Challenges in OECD Countries", *OECD Social, Employment and Migration Working Papers,* 79, OECD Publishing, Paris, http://dx.doi.org/10.1787/225505346577.

Commissariat Général au Développement Durable (2014), *Observatoire National des Emplois et Métiers de l'Économie Verte: Rapport d'Activité 2013*, Ministère de l'Écologie, du Développement Durable et de l'Énergie, Paris.

Commission of the European Communities (2009), *New Skills for New Jobs: Anticipating and Matching Labour Market and Skills Needs*, COM(2008) 868 Final, Brussels.

DAMVAD (2014), *Forecasting Future Needs for Advanced ICT Competence in Norway*, DAMVAD, Oslo, available at: http://www.damvad.com/media/101353/english-summary.pdf (accessed 8 February, 2016).

Department for Education and Science Policy (2012), *Education and Research 2011-2016: A Development Plan*, Ministry of Education and Culture, Helsinki.

Department of Employment (2014a), *Skill Shortage Research Methodology*, Australian Government, Canberra, available at: http://docs.employment.gov.au/system/files/doc/other/skillshortagelistaus_0.pdf (accessed 8 February, 2016).

Department of Employment (2014b), *Skill Shortage List Australia 2013-14*, Australian Government, Canberra, available at: http://docs.employment.gov.au/system/files/doc/other/skillshortagelistaus_0.pdf (accessed 8 February, 2016).

EGFSN – Expert Group on Future Skills Needs (2010), *Future Skills Needs of Enterprise within the Green Economy in Ireland*, EGFSN, Dublin.

EGFSN (2006), *Future Skills Requirements of the Digital Media Industry: Implications for Ireland*, EGFSN, Dublin.

Government of Ireland (2013), *Progress Report on Growth and Employment in the Green Economy in Ireland*, Government of Ireland, Dublin.

Government of Ireland (2012), *Delivering our Green Potential: Government Policy Statement on Growth and Employment in the Green Economy*, Government of Ireland, Dublin.

Humpl, S. and D. Bacher (2012), "The AMS-Skills Barometer: A Web-Based Labour-Market Tool, Making Use of Forecast Results by Stakeholders", *Building on Skills Forecasts – Comparing Methods and Applications, Conference Proceedings*, Research Paper, No. 18, CEDEFOP, pp. 82-96.

Immigration New Zealand (2014a), *Reviewing the Essential Skills in Demand Lists*, Wellington: Ministry of Business, Innovation and Employment, available at: http://www.immigration.govt.nz/migrant/general/generalinformation/review.htm (accessed 8 February, 2016).

Immigration New Zealand (2014b), *Long Term Skill Shortage List – June 2014*, Ministry of Business, Innovation and Employment, Wellington.

Norwegian Ministry for Education and Research (2010), *Science for the Future: Strategy for Strengthening Mathematics, Science and Technology (MST) 2010-1014*, Norwegian Ministry for Education and Research, Oslo.

Norwegian Ministry for Education and Research (2006), *A Joint Promotion of Mathematics, Science and Technology (MST): Strategy 2006-2009*, Norwegian Ministry for Education and Research, Oslo.

OECD (2015), *OECD Economic Surveys: New Zealand 2015,* OECD Publishing, Paris, http://dx.doi.org/10.1787/eco_surveys-nzl-2015-en.

OECD (2014a), "Background Paper prepared by the OECD", *G20-OECD-EC Conference on Quality Apprenticeships for Giving Youth a Better Start in the Labour Market*, OECD Conference Centre, Paris, 9 April 2014, available at: http://www.oecd.org/els/emp/G20-OECD-EC%20Apprenticeship%20Conference_Issues%20Paper.pdf (accessed 8 February, 2016).

OECD (2014b), *OECD Skills Strategy: Action Report Norway*, OECD, Paris.

OECD (2014c), *Matching Economic Migration with Labour Market Needs*, OECD Publishing, Paris, http://dx.doi.org/10.1787/9789264216501-en.

OECD (2011), *Towards Green Growth*, OECD Green Growth Studies, OECD Publishing, Paris, http://dx.doi.org/10.1787/9789264111318-en.

Pôle Emploi (2011a), "Les Emplois de la Croissance Verte, Enquête auprès des Employeurs", *Repères et Analyses*, Vol. 20.

Pôle Emploi (2011b), "Les Emplois de la Croissance Verte, Enquête auprès des Demandeurs d'Emploi", *Repères et Analyses*, Vol. 29.

Ruhs, M. and B. Anderson (eds.), (2010), *Who Needs Migrant Workers? Labour Shortages, Immigration and Public Policy*, Oxford University Press, Oxford.

UKCES (2011), *NOS Strategy 2010-2020,* UK Commission for Employment and Skills, London.

Chapter 4

Governance and stakeholder involvement

In this chapter, the various ways in which skills anticipation and assessment exercises may be governed are highlighted as well as the mechanisms put in place in countries for involving stakeholders in the discussion of findings and the development of a policy response. Governance of the exercises range from those that are user/policy-driven (and tend to be narrower in scope) to those that rely on independent agencies to produce assessments and forecasts for a more general use. Similarly, different approaches exist for stakeholder involvement, ranging from ad-hoc arrangements to more formal approaches. Either way, systems or procedures for dealing with potential conflict about skills needs or the required policy response are highly advisable.

Chapter 3 showed that stakeholder involvement and co-ordination is a key barrier preventing the information from skills assessment and anticipation exercises from being used further in policy making. A second barrier is the distance between the characteristics of the information produced by skills assessment and anticipation exercises and the needs of policy makers – a challenge that can be overcome by better co-ordinating the development process with the expected use. This chapter reviews how stakeholders are involved in: developing skills assessment and anticipation exercises; discussing the results; and developing a policy response. The chapter shows that involving different stakeholders, while necessary, is not a sufficient condition to guarantee consensus – and how this may limit the effective use of such information in policy making. The chapter also reviews the mechanisms put in place to build consensus on skills needs and to develop a policy response.

Main findings

- Governance of skills assessment and anticipation exercises can be understood as being oriented towards specific policy objectives (the *policy model*), completely independent of any policy objective (the *independent model*) or somewhere in between these two models. Both have advantages and disadvantages which can be overcome by better linking stakeholders and potential users of the exercises with the instrument-development process.
- In most countries, several actors are involved in the development of skills assessment and anticipation exercises. They commonly include different ministries, public employment services, regional- or sector-specific institutions, and social partners.
- These stakeholders are also generally involved in the discussion of the results and the development of a policy response. Stakeholder involvement can be considered an element of a well-designed skills assessment and anticipation exercise. In most countries, however, stakeholder involvement has led to disagreements about what the skill needs are and what the appropriate policy response is. There are also disagreements on the level of involvement as it is considered insufficient by the stakeholders themselves.
- Stakeholder involvement works best when high-level political engagement underpins the discussions. Discussion is also more fluid when the information on current or future skill needs comes from independent and well-reputed organisations or when there is a national skills strategy around which to centre the discussions.
- Formal mechanisms to facilitate the discussions include the existence of legal norms governing consultation around skills issues, the inclusion of stakeholders in advisory boards to different ministries, or a third party in charge of leading and co-ordinating the discussion around current or future skill needs.
- Informal mechanisms to facilitate consensus and conflict resolution include the setting up of work groups or round tables. They work best when the objectives of the discussion is directed towards specific and clear objectives with a realistic time line.

Stakeholder and government involvement

The involvement and collaboration of relevant actors can ensure that: i) the exercise is designed in such a way as to meet the needs of its users; ii) a consensus is reached about skills needs; and iii) the policy responses adopted across actors are coherent and complementary. One of the reported strengths of Norway's skills assessment and anticipation exercises, to cite just one example, is that employment and education authorities are involved in the design and development of the Statistics Norway forecasts, which ensures that they understand the outputs and use them for policy making. Similarly, analysts from the Flanders's (Belgium) public employment service involved in the anticipation exercises also sit on the decision-making bodies. It results in evidence being considered more fully and accurately in the development of employment policies and programmes.

Several governments have recognised the role employer organisations and trade unions can play in the development of skills assessment and anticipation exercises, as well as in the development and implementation of policies to respond to changing skills needs. Some countries have encouraged the creation of dedicated councils and committees to discuss skills needs identification exercises and skills policies. Such is the experience of Australia, Canada, Denmark, Estonia, Finland, France, Germany, Portugal, the Slovak Republic and the United Kingdom, for example. Employers have an active role in the skills assessment and anticipation exercises in Australia and New Zealand, as well as in Hungary (trade unions have a more modest role in Hungary). In Canada, human resources and skills-focused industry partnership organisations, including more than 20 Sector Councils (linking stakeholders from the business, labour and education communities, among others) examine current and projected skills needs. These organisations then help in the design and implementation of policies to assist firms and workers in adjusting to current and future skill needs (Commission of the European Communities, 2009; Box 4.1 provides more details on skills councils).

Box 4.1. **Skills councils**

Skills councils are employer-led or tri-partite organisations involving representatives from employers, workers and government or educational institutions. They are generally publicly funded, but can receive some additional funding from its private sector members. Several countries have established such sectoral councils (either national or regional), commissions or committees. Skills councils are usually independent organisations that provide a platform for the discussion of skills-related challenges of specific sectors or regional areas, as well as the development of joint policy responses. They provide recommendations on education and labour market policy, which can be general in nature, or specific to a certain region, sector or individual education and training institution and its programmes. One of their tasks is to monitor the labour market in the relevant sector and forecast which skills will be needed. These councils are generally involved in the provision of training, thus translating their sector-specific knowledge into education and training.

In the United Kingdom, for example, sector skills councils are employer-led organisations that define occupational standards and job competencies. This information helps firms from the respective sector identify the skills and corresponding qualifications needed for a particular job. Skills councils are also instrumental in organising apprenticeships and facilitating the linkage between training providers and firms, for the latter to engage in apprenticeships.

In Finland, there are 26 National Education and Training committees, representing different sectors of economic activity. They are tripartite bodies established by the Ministry of Education and Culture for a term of three years. Each committee acts as an expert body to anticipate skills and competence needs for the Ministry of Education and Culture and the Finnish National Board of Education.

The European Commission, as part of its Agenda for New Skills and Jobs, supports the setting up of European Sector Skills Councils to anticipate the skills needs in specific sectors more effectively and achieve a better match between skills and labour market needs. The councils will provide more and better information about the skills situation in different sectors. They will help develop skills governance in each sector and national skills policies by encouraging: national organisations to cater more effectively to the needs of the various sectors; organisations active in the same field to learn from each other; and all organisations concerned to share information and experience (European Commission, 2010).

Source: European Commission (2010), *New Skills for New Jobs: Policy Initiatives in the Field of Education*, Education, Audiovisual and Culture Executive Agency, Brussels.

Involvement in the development of skills assessment and anticipation exercises

The information from skills assessment and anticipation exercises is used by multiple actors. Their involvement in the development of the exercises can ensure that the design of the instruments meets their needs and that the information produced is best suited for its intended use.

The complexity of skills assessment and anticipation exercises may entail the need for substantial co-operation across different stakeholders. Figure 4.1 shows that the Ministries of Labour and Education, the statistical offices and employer organisations are the actors most frequently involved in skills assessment, forecast and foresight exercises. Universities/research centres/think tanks, trade unions, the public employment services (PES) and sector skills councils are also involved in almost 50% of countries or more. In contrast, private employment agencies, the ministries in charge of the environment and the national central banks are rarely involved in the development of these exercises. Although ministries in charge of migration are regular users of the information from skills assessment and anticipation exercises, they are rarely involved in the development of the exercises themselves.

Figure 4.1. **Government and stakeholder involvement in the development of skills assessment and anticipation exercises**

As a percentage of all countries

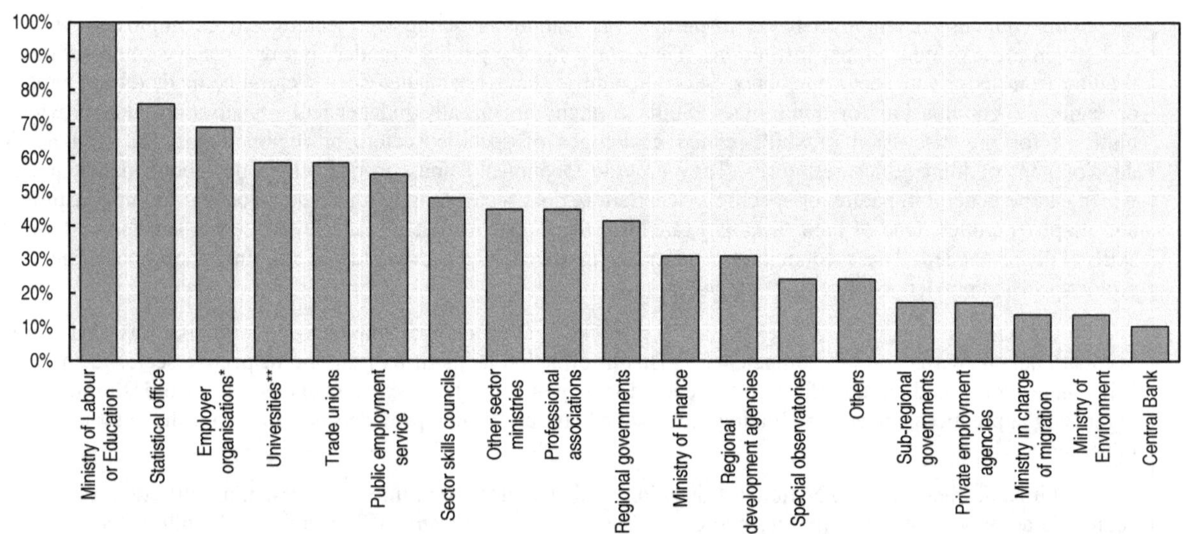

* Includes individual employers.

** Includes think tanks and research centres.

Note: Percentages based on responses from 28 countries reporting at least one involved actor (Australia, Austria, Belgium, Canada, Chile, the Czech Republic, Denmark, Estonia, Finland, France, Germany, Greece, Hungary, Ireland, Italy, Japan, Korea, the Netherlands, Norway, Poland, Portugal, the Slovak Republic, Slovenia, Spain, Sweden, Switzerland, Turkey and the United States). If more than one questionnaire was received per country, involvement is considered if reported in any questionnaire received.

Source: Questionnaire on Anticipating and Responding to Changing Skill Needs: Ministry of Labour and Ministry of Education questionnaires.

StatLink http://dx.doi.org/10.1787/888933334023

The three models of governance of skills assessment and anticipation exercises

Three main models of governance of skills assessment and anticipation exercises can be identified: the "independent model", the "policy model" and the "hybrid model". In the policy model, the exercises are developed directly by those actors who use the information to develop policies and programmes. In the independent model, they are led and developed by agencies that are independent of the users of the information and any policy objective. Finally, the hybrid model is a mixture of these two models.

In the independent model, the skills assessment and anticipation exercises are typically led and carried out by independent agencies. They are commonly the statistical office (e.g. Norway and Sweden) or universities/research institutes (e.g. ROA in the Netherlands or Denmark's DREAM model). Statistics Norway leads and carries out two exercises; agencies and stakeholders who finance or use the information from these exercises are members of the advisory board (e.g. Ministries, employer organisations, trade unions). In the Netherlands, although employer organisations would like to be involved in the development of the forecast, they recognise ROA's independence and the consequent stability in the methods used as an asset of the exercise. As discussed in Chapter 3, one risk with the independent model is that the level of aggregation and characteristics of the output are not necessarily useful for actors interested in using the information for policy-making purposes. For example, the output might be too technical, the level of aggregation not detailed enough at the sector or regional level, or skills definitions not easily translated to policy levers.

In the second approach to governance, the policy model, skills assessment and anticipation exercises are led by the end users of the information. Such exercises include those led by the public employment services. Across Europe, over half of PES monitor the structure of labour demand, skill requirements, mix of job vacancies and how it relates to the composition of jobseekers. The majority of PES in Europe also make an effort to estimate future training needs. In Denmark, the Danish Agency for Labour Market and Recruitment estimates labour mismatches and shortages for over 1 000 occupations across four regions (Manoudi et al., 2014). The PES in Austria, Belgium (Flanders and Wallonia), France, Poland, Sweden and Turkey develop their own skills assessment and anticipation exercises to inform their policies and practices (see Box 4.2 for the role of public employment services in enabling skills assessment and anticipation information to have a positive impact on the labour market).

This model also includes those exercises led by the agencies in charge of vocational education and training (e.g. the National Agency for Qualification and Vocational Education and Training, ANQEP in Portugal), by the agencies developing occupational standards and qualification frameworks (e.g. ChileValora in Chile and Portugal public employment service, IEEP), or by universities seeking to define the number of vacancies to offer in the short- and medium-term (e.g. Austrian and Swedish higher education institutions). In these cases, the exercises are designed to answer very specific policy-related issues and can actively engage and use input from stakeholders around a specific objective. Being so focused on one particular objective, however, may lead exercises under this governance model to lack the flexibility or broadness in scope to be applicable or useful by other actors.

Box 4.2. **Public Employment Services (PES) and the links with employers**

Public employment services (PES) are important actors enabling skills assessment and anticipation information to have a positive impact on the labour market. They can direct skill development and active labour market policies to sectors in higher demand. In most countries, PES have the aim of connecting jobseekers with employers and to help match the supply and demand of skills on the labour market through the dissemination of information, training, placement and active support services at local, national and supranational level. PES occupy a strategic position, as they can use general skills assessment and forecast information to implement local policies. For this to happen, however, PES need to be given the flexibility, capacity and autonomy to be able to drive these national/regional policy orientations to effective policies and programmes for jobseekers and employers at the local level (Froy et al., 2011).

An efficient skills anticipation strategy also requires close co-operation between PES activities, on the one hand, and employers and jobseekers, on the other, to ensure that policy responses based on skills information are adequately implemented. Andersen et al. (2010) find that most PES emphasise the importance of maintaining a close dialogue with employers and their organisations. Despite its importance, however, the dialogue between PES and employers is in some cases not systematic and it involves only a smaller subset of employers. Most PES co-operate on an informal basis with sector organisations to discuss the trends in, and prospects for, the sector. Only a few PES collaborate with employer organisations in the design and development of analyses of future skill requirements, and even fewer PES report that they participated in a formal partnership with employer organisations. Exceptions to this trend include Latvia (Bartlett, 2013), Austria, Belgium, France, Sweden and Turkey, where to facilitate the activation of skills and job search, PES are in charge of skill needs assessment and forecast exercises.

Some PES, like the *Vlaamse Dienst voor Arbeidsbemiddeling en Beroepsopleiding* [VDAB, Belgium's (Flanders) public employment service], have begun to adopt skills profiling in characterising jobseekers to facilitate matches, assess jobseekers' risk of unemployment and better inform the needs of jobseekers. Through skills profiling, PES capture and describe a jobseeker's potential in terms of "generic" and "soft" skills and require employers to include more detailed information on skill requirements in their vacancies (including technical, generic and soft skills). There is currently little evidence to support the potential gains from skills profiling, but feedback from country studies suggest a growing body of evidence to shows that skills profiling result in an increased exit rate from unemployment, a reduction in the number of long-term unemployed, a reduction in the average duration of unemployment, and increased satisfaction on the part of jobseekers and employers (Blázquez, 2014). *Arbeitsmarktservice Österreich* (Austria's PES) is planning to incorporate such skills-based matching in its job-matching programmes.

Source: Andersen et al. (2010), "Anticipating Skill Needs of the Labour Force and Equipping People for New Jobs, Which role for Public Employment Services in Early Identification of Skill Needs and Labour Up-Skilling?", Final report prepared under contract to the European Commission, Directorate General for Employment, Social Affairs and Equal Opportunities; Bartlett, W. (2013), "Structural Unemployment in the Western Balkans: Challenges for Skills Anticipation and Matching Policies", *European Planning Studies*, Vol. 21, No. 6, pp. 890-908; Blázquez, M. (2014), Skills-Based Profiling and Matching in PES, Publications Office of the European Union, Luxembourg; Froy, F. et al. (2011), "Building Flexibility and Accountability into Local Employment Services: Synthesis of OECD Studies in Belgium, Canada, Denmark and the Netherlands", *OECD Local Economic and Employment Development (LEED) Working Papers*, Vol. 2011/10, OECD Publishing, Paris, http://dx.doi.org/10.1787/5kg3mkv3tr21-en.

In this regard, Portugal shows collaboration across different stakeholders in two separate skills needs analyses that are geared towards specific policy objectives: one for the development of qualifications frameworks and another for directing VET policy. The update of the National Catalogue of Qualifications (CNQ) is managed through the collaboration of 16 Sector Councils for Qualifications (CSQ) which, co-ordinated by ANQEP, cover all sectors of economic activity. The CSQ integrate a heterogeneous set of stakeholders that include social partners, education and training providers (e.g. public high schools, vocational schools, vocational training centres and private certified training providers), key employers in the respective sector, technology and innovation centres, sector regulators and corresponding professional associations. In addition to the appointed members (and depending on the issues to be discussed), invited experts may also attend the meetings of the CSQ. The co-operation across stakeholders is extensive and all represented bodies in the CSQ can make proposals for the integration of new qualifications in the CNQ, or the restructuring or elimination of existing qualifications. This can be done using an online tool (Open Model of Consultation) which is available at any time to the CSQ members.

Exercises led by employer organisations or individual employers also fall under the policy model of governance. This approach is less common, however, given that skills assessment and anticipation exercises exist in all countries and employers therefore do not see the value added of building their own models. In Canada, one notable exception is the initiative of a large industrial employer and sectoral organisations, such as: Buildforce Canada, the Petroleum Human Resources Council, the Mining Human Resources Council, Trucking HR Canada, that carries out their own skills assessments and anticipation exercises to inform the location of facilities, to develop training programmes and apprenticeships, and inform workers about skills needs. Also, in Chile, large employers in the mining sector created a sectoral employer organisation, the *Consejo Minero de Chile* (Chilean Mining Council). Since 2011, and possibly in response to the need for skills anticipation information, this council has produced ten-year skills forecasts taking into account the projected medium-term investments of each firm as well as labour supply and demand forecasts. These results are then used in collaboration with education and training providers in the mining region to determine training courses and orient VET curricula in upper secondary schools. In France, an employer organisation has recently launched a skills needs assessment and, in Japan, a large employer (that is not involved in the government-led exercises) carries out its own annual national skills assessment based on employer and worker/graduate surveys to inform its human resource policy.

In between the policy and the independent model a third, the hybrid model. It covers exercises that are led by ministries (and with a clear policy orientation), yet remain relatively independent of their ultimate use. Examples of exercises that fall under this model include those carried out by national ministries in federal countries (e.g. Canada's COPS model, Australia's current skills assessment and forecasts, Germany's BIBB-IAB Qualifications and Occupational Fields forecasts and the United States' Bureau of Labor Statistics projections) or carried out by national ministries with the close collaboration of public employment services and other government or non-government actors (e.g. Austria and Australia's Skills Shortage List). Other examples are those exercises led by skills councils (e.g. Australia, Canada and Ireland), given that skills councils are independent bodies that provide recommendations for other actors to decide on and implement policies and programmes (see Box 4.1 on skills councils).

Inter-ministerial collaboration in developing a policy response

Skills policies involve action in both the areas of skill demand and skill supply, therefore spanning the responsibilities of several ministries. The two ministries most likely to be involved are the Ministries of Education and Labour. Other ministries (e.g. sector-specific or the ministry in charge of migration) may also be involved. Skills assessment and anticipation information therefore represents an important input policy makers can use to link skill supply to skill demand to formulate consistent and coherent employment, migration, education and/or economic policies. As discussed in Chapter 3, results from skills assessment and anticipation exercises are used by several ministries. Given the inter-ministerial nature of skills policy, the development of these policies could benefit from the joint involvement of more than one ministry in the discussion of the results and in the development of the corresponding policy responses. This can help the development of coherent policies across government agencies.

In practically all countries, more than one ministry is involved in both the discussion of the results of skills assessment and anticipation exercises, and in the development of a corresponding policy response. Inter-ministerial participation tends to involve the Ministries of Education and Labour. Figure 4.2 shows the extent to which different ministries are involved in the discussion of the results from skills assessment and anticipation exercises. The ministries involved also include the Ministry of Economy, the Treasury, the Ministry of Health (or Social Affairs), the ministry in charge of migration or foreign affairs, and the ministry in charge of environment. Table 4.1 provides a further breakdown by country of the information presented in Figure 4.2. In the majority of countries, three or more ministries are involved.

Figure 4.2. **Involvement of ministries in discussing results from skills assessment and anticipation exercises or in developing a policy response**

As a percentage of all countries

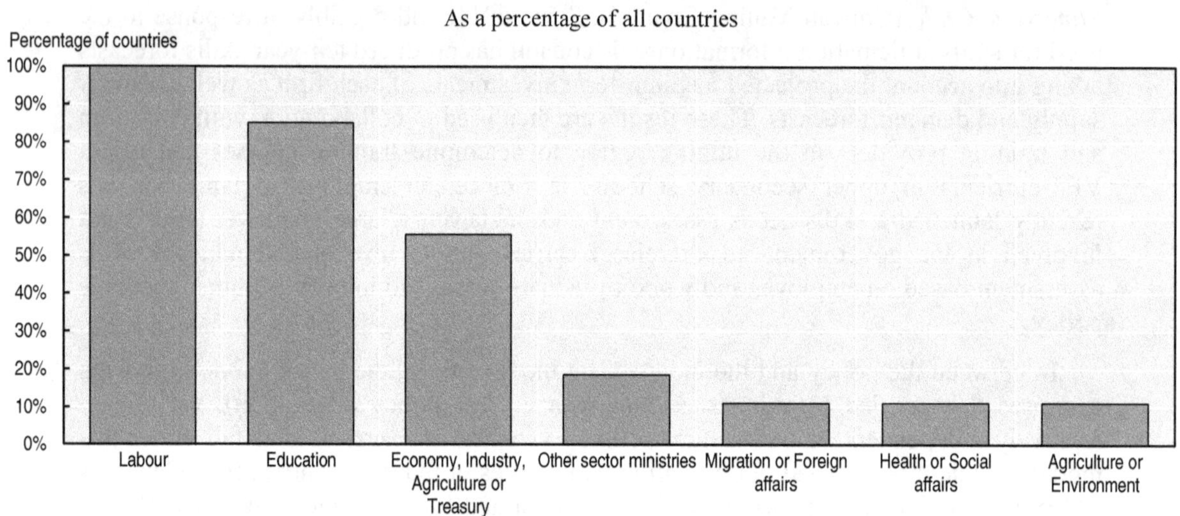

Note: Percentages based on responses from 26 countries that identified at least one ministry as involved (Australia, Austria, Belgium, Canada, Chile, the Czech Republic, Estonia, Finland, France, Germany, Hungary, Ireland, Italy, Japan, Korea, the Netherlands, Norway, Poland, Portugal, the Slovak Republic, Slovenia, Spain, Sweden, Switzerland, Turkey and the United States). If more than one questionnaire was received per country, involvement is considered if reported in any questionnaire received.

Source: Questionnaire on Anticipating and Responding to Changing Skill Needs: Ministry of Labour and Ministry of Education questionnaires.

StatLink http://dx.doi.org/10.1787/888933334032

Inter-ministerial collaboration appears absent in Japan because exercises were designed and are used for very specific policy objectives (e.g. informing public employment service activity, VET programme and curriculum development). In Poland, the discussions of results from skills assessment and anticipation exercises, and the development of the corresponding policy response, take place only within the Ministry of Labour and Social Policy. Any collaboration that does take place, does so in the context of a broader-based inter-ministerial group for lifelong learning. However, a new forecasting exercise is being developed which will spur inter-ministerial collaboration.

Table 4.1. **Inter-ministerial collaboration, by country**

	Education	Labour	Economy, Industry, Agriculture or Treasury	Migration or Foreign Affairs	Health or Social Affairs	Other sector ministries	Agriculture or Environment
Australia		X	X	X			
Austria	X	X	X				
Belgium (Flanders)	X	X					
Belgium (Wallonia)	X	X					
Canada		X	X	X	X	X	
Chile	X	X	X				
Czech Republic	X	X					
Estonia	X	X					
Finland	X	X	X				
France	X	X			X		X
Germany	X	X	X				
Hungary	X	X	X				X
Ireland	X	X	X				
Italy	X	X					
Japan		X					
Korea	X	X	X			X	
Netherlands	X	X	X				
Norway	X	X	X		X	X	
Poland		X					
Portugal	X	X	X			X	
Slovak Republic	X	X	X				X
Slovenia	X	X					
Spain	X	X					
Sweden	X	X	X				
Switzerland	X	X		X			
Turkey	X	X	X			X	
United States	X	X					

Note: Only the 26 countries that replied to either the Ministry of Labour or the Ministry of Education and indicated the ministries involved are included. If a ministry is mentioned in either questionnaire it is marked as involved. In some countries, Education and Labour (or other ministries) are hosted under the same ministry; in these cases the involvement of different sectoral agencies within the ministry is considered (e.g. Finland, Ireland, Slovak Republic and Switzerland). Denmark replied that inter-ministerial collaboration takes place but did not provide details on the specific ministries involved.

Source: Questionnaire on Anticipating and Responding to Changing Skill Needs: Ministry of Labour and Ministry of Education questionnaires.

StatLink http://dx.doi.org/10.1787/888933334056

The mechanisms to co-ordinate inter-ministerial collaboration vary across countries. In Australia, Estonia, Flanders (Belgium), the Netherlands and Sweden, collaboration is not systematic, but occurs through informal meetings or on an *ad-hoc* basis. Despite this, these countries tend to have quite a longstanding tradition of effective inter-ministerial collaboration. In Austria, Canada, Switzerland the United States, discussions take place in the context of inter-ministerial skills committees (e.g. the New Skills Initiative in Austria; the Initiative for Qualified Labour in Switzerland; the Skills Working Group in the United States; and the Economic Trends and Policies Committee and the Social Trends, Policies and Institutions Committee in Canada). The United States' Skills Working Group, formed in 2014, brings together 13 federal agencies and the White House. Each agency has a designated contact point. In addition to this working group, inter-ministerial collaboration in the United States takes place through *ad-hoc* meetings based around specific skills issues that bring together only the relevant agencies.

In Chile, Ireland, Italy, Finland, Norway, Portugal and Spain, inter-ministerial collaboration takes place more indirectly through a third-party, independent body or work programme. This third party receives the advice and feedback from the ministries. However, as Turkey reports, this collaboration may be limited if ministry representatives have no continuity from meeting to meeting. Some of the bodies that bring together ministries within each country include ChileValora in Chile, Hungary's National Body of VET Qualifications, Turkey's Vocational Training Council, the Higher Technical Institutes (*Istituti Tecnici Superiori*, ITS) in Italy, the governance of forecast exercises in Norway and Finland and the governance of the National Agency for Qualification and Vocational Education and Training (ANQEP) in Portugal. Ireland's Expert Group on Future Skill Needs is an independent body that reports the Ministry of for Jobs, Entreprise and Innovation and to the Ministry of Education and Skills. Its mandate calls it to advise the Irish Government on current and future skills needs of the economy. It takes a central role in ensuring that labour market needs for skilled workers are anticipated and met. In Spain, inter-ministerial collaboration takes place in the General Council for Vocational Training, which brings together representatives from the ministries of education and labour, as well as VET stakeholders. Collaboration in Spain also takes place through general and regular inter-ministerial meetings or *ad-hoc* working groups.

Collaboration across regional/sub-regional administrative levels and other government agencies

The development and implementation of policies in response to skills assessment and anticipation exercises involves a regional and local dimension as well (OECD, 2014). As emphasised by the European Commission (2013), "the tasks of regional governments include, among others: defining and co-operating in the field of regional labour market policy, co-ordination (at regional scale) of tasks in the field of vocational guidance, vocational information, lifelong learning and active labour market programmes, initialising and implementation of pilot projects, etc." Involving actors from different regional/sub-regional administrative levels may help validate the results of skills assessment and anticipation exercises at the local and sector level. It also adds nuance to the conclusions reached and brings flexibility in the corresponding policy response. Furthermore, the introduction of multi-level governance systems in many OECD countries, spurred the vertical relationships between players at different levels[1] in both the identification of policy targets and in the formulation of policy responses. National ministries are nowadays increasingly required to design policy interventions in collaboration with regional and local authorities by mixing top-down and bottom-up decision-making strategies. At regional/local level, for instance, information about the future supply of, and demand for, skills is used for planning purposes – such as the setting of production targets, development of action plans, budgeting and distribution of resources to local skills programmes (see Box 4.3 for an example).

Certain national governments involve regional and sub-regional authorities in the discussion of results from skills assessment and anticipation exercises, and/or in the development of the corresponding policy response. In most cases, national governments involve actors from the regional level. Only Canada, Italy and Portugal involve actors from the sub-regional level. In Canada, the Forum of Labour Market Ministers is another mechanism for collaboration. It is co-chaired by the Minister of ESDC and includes ministers from all provinces and territories, is involved in discussing skills assessments, forecasts and other related issues. The national level is completely absent from the discussions in Norway and Belgium, as discussions are held at the regional level only.

In Belgium this is a direct result of the fact that education, labour market and employment policy are the responsibility of each region. Nevertheless, in Belgium, public vocational training providers from the three regions have set up *Synerjob,* a concerted platform for their activities. Regional administrative levels are not involved in the discussion of results in Switzerland, Chile or Slovenia. In general, the development of a policy response involves the same actors in all countries, except Japan, France, the Czech Republic and Switzerland, where regional governments take part in the discussions of results, but not in the development of a policy response. In Italy and Canada, sub-regional governments do not take part in the national policy response but they are involved in the development of a local policy response. In most countries, then, the local policy response is developed without the involvement of sub-regional governments.

Box 4.3. **An example of skills anticipation activity at the regional level: Slovenia**

How skills anticipation information is used depends of the specific objectives of the users (e.g. whether they are ministries, local authorities or end users such as employers or jobseekers). Regional occupational advisors in Slovenia monitor enrolment in (upper) secondary school programmes in their area, the enrolment of students in further education programmes, and how many graduates and what type of graduates are joining the labour market. This information feeds into schools, particularly those running vocational education programmes, and to skills matching policies. Advisors working at the regional level play a double role. On the one hand, they collect information about current and future skills supply and demand by analysing their local labour market and education infrastructure. This information helps set up policy targets. It also helps the policy discussion and formulation with other public administration agencies (such as ministries). The information on skill supply and demand is also passed to employers looking for workers (especially in areas with skills deficits) (Andersen, 2010).

Source: Andersen, T. et al. (2010), "Anticipating Skill Needs of the Labour Force and Equipping People for New Jobs. Which Role for Public Employment Services in Early Identification of Skill Needs and Labour Up-Skilling?", Final report prepared under contract to the European Commission, Directorate General for Employment, Social Affairs and Equal Opportunities.

According to ministry responses, two reasons explain the lack of involvement of sub-regional governments in the development of a national policy response. First, they lack the capacity or flexibility to engage in the development of a policy response. Second, there is no body to co-ordinate the regional/sub-regional governments' involvement. In the federalist context of the Swiss administration, streamlining policies at a national level does not make much economic sense (although there are permanent bodies that co-ordinate health, education, finance, labour market and economic policies across cantons). In Canada, the fact that results from some exercises (e.g. COPS) are not available at such a disaggregated level limits the possibility of involving sub-regional entities. In the United States, state governments tend to change their priorities and resources frequently, making it difficult to maintain a continuous dialogue with the federal government. In Spain, by Constitutional decree, education is the remit of each Autonomous Community; the central government sets the basic framework and can only co-operate with the communities (not co-ordinate policy across administrative levels). In Chile and Turkey, sub-regional governments play a bigger role in implementing policies developed at a higher administrative level, but not in the development of the policy response itself. In Ireland, the lack of capacity and absence of a body to co-ordinate regional governments is being overcome by the creation of bodies chaired by the local authorities to assist in the co-ordination of local responses to skill needs and a rationalisation of the sub-national governance system (MacCarthaigh, 2013). In Hungary, discussions were previously held at the regional level but these discussions have recently been devolved to the county (i.e. sub-regional) level. The idea is that by devolving the discussions to a local level, the quality of the discussions will improve as will the capacity to adapt them to local labour market needs.A variety of other government agencies can also be involved. Public Employment Services (PES) – which are already carrying out exercises in some countries – can participate in the identification of policy targets, or be consulted on the definition of policy objectives. The Finnish PES, for example, has the mandate to collaborate closely with the Ministry of Employment and the Economy (European Commission, 2013). As described above, Belgian, Austrian, Polish and Swedish PES play a leading role in carrying out skills assessment and anticipation exercises. They also play a leading role in the discussions and in developing uses of this information.

Collaboration with social partners and other stakeholders

Since the beginning of the Copenhagen Process in 2002, European member states have increased their involvement in skills anticipation initiatives. "Several new bodies have been established or enlarged, social partners' functions have been expanded, educational acts and training regulations have been modernised answering the new needs and challenges of the labour market" (CEDEFOP, 2008, p. 23). Anticipating future skills needs has, since then, become a priority across the activities carried out by a variety of different social partners and stakeholders.

In practically all countries, employer organisations, trade unions and VET providers are invited to discuss findings, but these stakeholders are involved in fewer countries in the development of the policy response. In the majority of countries professional associations, general education providers and sector skills councils are also invited to both the discussion of findings and the development of a policy response. The invitation of these actors to the development of a policy response is always less common than the invitation to discuss the findings (Figure 4.3). Most often, employer organisations are invited to update occupational and qualification standards, or to design/revise active labour market policies or labour market regulation. Trade union confederations are invited to design/revise initial training programmes or qualifications, and to update occupational standards or qualifications frameworks. Involvement usually takes place through sector skills councils, where they exist (see Box 4.1). In Canada, for example, sector skill councils have been instrumental in the design of national occupational standards and certification programmes (Commission of the European Communities, 2009). In the Czech Republic, sector skills councils work towards the definition of qualification frameworks. In Estonia they develop occupational standards that are then used in curriculum design. In Australia they lead skills anticipation exercises and provide direct input for policy action.

Ensuring high quality involvement of the social partners facilitates smooth feedback between the actors. An employer organisation in Norway, for example, mentions that it is regularly invited to tri-partite committees to discuss results from skills assessment and anticipation exercises and to discuss the appropriate policy response. Yet, it also reports that their influence (low) in these committees is not proportional to their involvement (high). Social partners in Germany are generally involved as advisors to government programmes. Ireland's Ministry of Education and Skills recognises that a lack of engagement on the part of employers and of resources to promote this engagement limits social partners' involvement in the discussions. Korea's social partners, experts, and human resource development committees are brought together in the Vocational Training Innovation Review and Assessment Committee. Canada's COPS forecasts initially invited professional associations to the discussions, but given their low engagement, the invitation was discontinued. The agency leading COPS recognises the need to promote social partners' engagement and creates spaces for interaction and engagement through workshops like the "Skills Summit". In Spain, stakeholders are involved in the General Council for Vocational Training, the State school board and the University Council; collaboration with stakeholders is hindered by their lack of interest and the fact that more than 95% of Spanish firms are SMEs. Social partner involvement in Chile, Estonia and Turkey is limited by the weak organisational capacity of sectoral organisations: they do not have the legitimacy to represent all members within the sector, or they lack the organisational capacity to influence or actually participate in the discussions. The difficulty to involve a representative set of social partners in the United States is due to the large size and diversity of its economy.

Figure 4.3. **Stakeholder involvement in the discussion of findings from skills assessment and anticipation exercises and the development of a policy response**

As a percentage of all countries

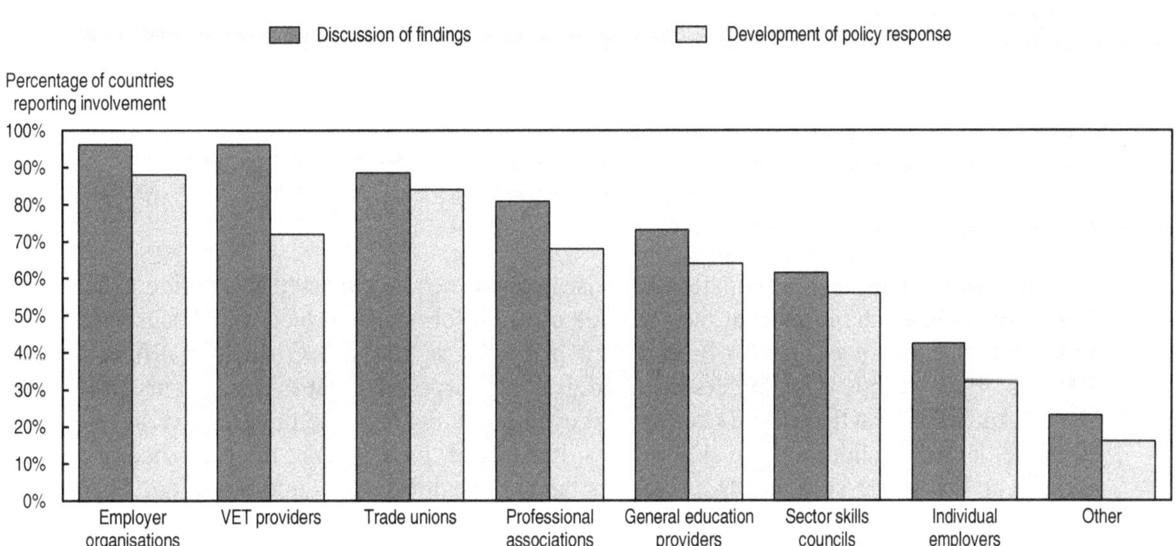

Note: Percentages for the discussion of findings based on responses from 25 countries reporting at least one stakeholder involved (Austria, Belgium, Canada, Chile, the Czech Republic, Denmark, Estonia, Finland, France, Germany, Hungary, Ireland, Italy, Korea, Japan, the Netherlands, Norway, Poland, Portugal, the Slovak Republic, Slovenia, Spain, Sweden, Switzerland and Turkey). Percentage for the development of a policy response based on responses from 24 countries reporting at least one stakeholder involved (Austria, Belgium, Canada, Chile, the Czech Republic, Denmark, Estonia, Finland, France, Germany, Hungary, Ireland, Italy, Japan, Korea, the Netherlands, Norway, Portugal, the Slovak Republic, Slovenia, Spain, Sweden, Switzerland and Turkey). If more than one questionnaire was received per country, involvement is considered if reported in any questionnaire received.

Source: Questionnaire on Anticipating and Responding to Changing Skill Needs: Ministry of Labour and Ministry of Education questionnaires.

StatLink http://dx.doi.org/10.1787/888933334041

One of the strengths of the Finnish skills assessment and anticipation system is its regular and systematic involvement of social partners. Social partners are, for example, involved in the interpretation of the results before their finalisation to allow for new analyses to be carried out if necessary to reach firmer conclusions and consensus. Social partners take part in the National Education and Training committees. They are sector-specific tri-partite organisations and act as an expert advisory body to the Ministry of Education and Culture and the Finnish National Board of Education. A different model is adopted in the context of Italy's *Instituti Tecnici Superiori* (ITS), whereby the systematic consultation with social partners and other stakeholders is regulated and ensured by an inter-ministerial decree.

Consensus reaching and mechanisms to resolve differences

Difficulty in reaching consensus: Some examples

As noted in the previous section, in most countries a series of ministries, government agencies, regional and sub-regional administrative levels and social partners are involved in the discussions of results from skills assessment and anticipation exercises. They are also involved in the development of an appropriate policy response. The number of actors as well as the diversity of interests and institutional objectives may make it difficult to reach consensus when deciding, first, what the skills needs are and, second, on the most appropriate policy response to these needs. Enabling dialogue between stakeholders is an obvious first step. It may be hindered, however, by the limited time availability from agencies and stakeholders to take part in conversations, by the changing priorities and resources of different agencies and by the need for agencies to find mutual benefits to collaboration and avoiding duplication of work. When collaboration takes place, however, agreement on skills needs and policy responses may still be difficult.

Difficulty in agreeing on skill needs

Skills assessment and anticipation exercises should not be expected to provide exact predictions of the future. Instead, they provide useful information to feed into discussions about future skills needs and where policy priorities should lie. Given the different interests of the various stakeholders involved, it is not surprising, that disagreements arise about what skills exactly will be needed, and even more so about the policies that should be implemented to address these skills issues. In Finland, for example, there has been no agreement on future skill needs in the social and health sector, nor has there been agreement between the government and the trade unions regarding the skill needs in some private service sectors like cleaning. There has also been disagreement across regional and sub-regional administrative levels regarding the distribution of VET vacancies to address skills needs.

While disagreements about skills needs and the policies needed to address them are to some extent normal, they can be exacerbated, in some cases, by: i) the very nature and design of the skills assessment and anticipation exercises; ii) an incomplete understanding of the scope of skills assessments and anticipation exercises; or iii) the lack of clarity in the interpretation of the results between the actors involved:

- The nature and design of the exercises can hinder consensus in skills needs where there are too many assessments that provide conflicting evidence (e.g. Denmark, France, Finland Greece or the Netherlands). In Greece, the large number of assessments and their irregular frequency make it hard for stakeholders to agree on skills needs. In Finland, regional skills assessment and anticipation exercises follow different methodologies, limiting the comparability of results and stakeholders' discussions.
- An incomplete understanding of the scope and characteristics of skills assessment and anticipation exercises can also lead to difficulty in agreeing on skill needs. This is the case when there are unrealistic expectations of what skills

assessment and anticipation exercises can (and cannot) do, or when findings from the exercises are not in accordance with the social partners' own perception of local skill needs [e.g. Canada, Finland and Flanders (Belgium)].

- Similarly, the results themselves can be interpreted in different ways by different actors. In Denmark, for example, the same findings produced divergent interpretations between trade unions and the government about the role of unskilled labour in the future (unions support the idea that unskilled labour will not be relevant in the future, while the Danish Government and the employers argue that unskilled labour will be demanded in the future).

Difficulty in agreeing on the appropriate policy response

Once skills needs are identified and potentially agreed upon, difficulties may also appear in agreeing on the appropriate policy response. Such differences have been evidenced in Norway, for example, in the debate around the need for more vocational as opposed to higher education, and in Estonia, where questions are raised about whether addressing skills needs should be achieved even if it means limiting student choice. These difficulties sometimes reflect the characteristics of social dialogue in a country more generally. They may also come as a result of the distribution of responsibilities in skills policy or a lack of political will to search for consensus. Most commonly, however, they are a result of the differing or even opposing interests across different stakeholders.

In France, Korea, Switzerland and Canada, for example, one barrier to agreeing on a policy response is the distribution of responsibilities when it comes to dealing with skills policy. Many actors are involved in skills policy development, and so it is hard for one to take a leading role in the policy response – unless this has been explicitly agreed amongst all partners. In Latvia and Estonia, a lack of political limits inter-ministerial collaboration. This limitation is compounded by a lack of recognition of the complexity and multi-sectoral nature of skills policy, hindering the search for policies based on consensus.

Conflicting interests by different stakeholders can also complicate the development of an agreed policy response. This has been the case in France, for example, where employer organisations and public officials favour short-term responses to skills needs, while trade unions prefer longer-term training responses that allow workers to transfer their skills across firms. Similarly, French employers tend to favour training that makes workers job-ready, while government authorities prefer the provision of more general skills. In Flanders (Belgium), Korea and the Netherlands, conflicting interests have risen across agencies within government as if they have different policy objectives or views on how to address a particular skill need. The engagement of different agencies in the United States is hindered by the need to align their different priorities and the need to develop co-ordinated strategies that work for each agency given their different interests and objectives. This is especially the case for agencies for which skills is not a priority, so their participation is harder to obtain.

Mechanisms to facilitate consensus and conflict resolution

Several mechanisms exist across countries to facilitate consensus-building and overcome potential conflict. These include involving stakeholders in the advisory boards of key agencies or actively involving them through thematic workshops. Dialogue and consensus-reaching is facilitated when skills needs information comes from an independent and well-regarded institution. A national skills strategy can facilitate discussions across stakeholders by framing discussions. Other consensus-reaching mechanisms include: consolidating the dialogue in a network or a central agency; developing a legal framework that articulates the engagement of different stakeholders in the process; involving high-level political representatives; and articulating the discussions around very concrete and short-term objectives.

With the intention of providing a platform for resolving conflict, Denmark involves stakeholders in advisory councils to different ministries. Trade unions and employer organisations are involved in the advisory boards of the regional and local education committees of Wallonia (Belgium), where they are also members of the public employment service's governing body. Participation of stakeholders in the agency carrying out the skills assessment exercises can ensure a common understanding of future skills needs and the long-term economic environment (e.g. Norway, Finland). In Ireland, independent bodies, the Expert Group on Future Skills Needs (EGFSN) and the Further Education and Training Authority (SOLAS), are in charge of skills assessment and anticipation exercises. Both EGFSN and SOLAS involve ministries, regional agencies and other public bodies. EGFSN also involves social partners and reports to the ministries of Employment and Education. Inter-ministerial collaboration (and collaboration with stakeholders) in employment and vocational training policies has improved in recent years in Portugal, largely due to the efforts of ANQEP, an agency established under the supervision of the Ministry of Education and Science and the Ministry of Solidarity Employment and Social Security, in co-operation with the Ministry of Economy (OECD, 2015). In Canada, and in response to the perplexities expressed by employers in response to official forecasts, the Department of Employment and Social Development (ESDC) has engaged with stakeholders directly or in *ad-hoc* workshops to provide a better understanding of the forecasts and what they can and cannot do. In Norway, narrowly-themed conferences promote consensus reaching, as was the case of a conference on skills needs in the engineering sector (carried out in April 2014) and another one on skills brought by immigrant workers (October 2014).

The success of stakeholder participation in key organisations is facilitated, in Finland, Denmark, Portugal, Sweden and Switzerland, by a long tradition of social dialogue, consensus-building and stakeholder involvement in discussions, which may not be easy to replicate in other countries in the short term. Having an independent and reputed organisation carry out skills assessment and anticipation exercises with a respected methodology is an asset to facilitate dialogue around the results, as is the case in Norway or Flanders (Belgium). A National Skills Strategy can act as a framework for consensus-building and for guiding the discussions around a common objective, as is the case in Austria, Germany, Ireland, Switzerland or the United States. A skills strategy is currently being developed in Portugal. The skills assessment and anticipation exercises in Korea are closely linked to the national strategic development plans and the national skills policy, framing the discussion in such a framework.

In Germany, social partners are generally involved in the advisory boards of government programmes. Discussions benefit from a longstanding tradition of co-operation between the social partners, even though disagreements exist. Working groups engaging several ministers, social partners, representatives from different administrative levels and academia are common-place. In addition, government regulations stipulate regular meetings across government agencies. As of the end of 2014, the German Alliance for Education and Training (*Allianz für Aus- und Weiterbildung*) brings together the Ministry of Economy, Education and Labour, regional governments and social partners to co-ordinate training strategies in Germany. The alliance is a broad social pact that, among other mandates, seeks to reduce skills mismatches and shortages. It provides an arena to discuss results from skills assessment and anticipation exercises, develop and co-ordinate the corresponding policy responses. It stipulates avenues for inter-ministerial and tri-partite discussions at different levels (at the level of Secretaries of States and Directors as well as a technical level). In parallel, the Ministry of Labour and Social Affairs has convened a partnership between several ministries and social partners and skills issues are a part of its agenda. Although education is not the remit of the federal government, at the state and local level the dual education system relies on the contribution of social partners and firms for its development, strengthening the involvement of different actors in the discussion of skill needs and the development of corresponding policy responses.

France, struggling with a scattered policy response and a large number of exercises in place, will move towards a more co-ordinated approach by establishing the *Réseau Emploi Compétences* (REC). It is a network that will articulate the discussions and the various exercises. Also in France, the two councils for employment and training involving stakeholders (and that enable discussions between them) have been merged into one: the *Conseil National de l'Emploi, de la Formation et de l'Orientation Professionnelles* (CNEFOP) (previously: the *Conseil National pour la Formation Professionnelle Tout au Long de la Vie* [CNFPTLV] and the *Conseil National de l'Emploi* [CNE]). The Central Training Council in Japan also articulates discussions about skills anticipation in the context of the training system across ministries, regional/sub-regional administrative levels and stakeholders. Both Estonia and Finland are developing a mechanism to better co-ordinate the different exercises and the instances for stakeholder collaboration (Nurmela, 2011).

In Italy, legal norms that govern inter-ministerial agreements make provisions for the systematic consultation with stakeholders in the definition of skill needs and in the development of policies to enhance the link between training and production chains. The Conference of the State, Regional Administrations and Autonomous provinces plays an important role in articulating agreements across regional/sub-regional administrative levels. Stakeholders are involved in VET providers' steering committees, ensuring that the skills provided are aligned with those required by employers. In the United States, the Workforce Innovation and Opportunity Act (WIOA), signed in 2014, consolidates job training programmes into a single funding stream. Among other provisions, it promotes greater and better consultation among federal agencies, in particular the Department of Labor and the Department of Education, and requires collaboration between agencies at the state level through joint strategic planning efforts. In the Netherlands, the agency in charge of implementing the employment insurance (UWV) is also in charge of providing labour and data services. Its mandate calls it to ensure transparency in the labour market, and that no barriers hinder the collaboration and co-ordination with stakeholders. The new skills assessment and anticipation exercise in the Czech Republic (PŘEKVAP) will include provisions for the organisation of dialogue between stakeholders. These provisions are a direct recognition of the importance and the challenge involved in reaching consensus.

Ensuring high-level political engagement facilitates collaboration across agencies and regional-sub-regional administrative levels in the United States. This has meant engaging agency heads (directors and ministers) in the discussions, both at the federal and regional (state) levels. It is one of the factors underpinning the successful collaboration in the Career Pathways programme in the United States'. It involved the Department of Education, the Department of Health and Human Services, the Department of Labour and regional and local governments to consolidate inter-sectoral training strategies and promote the transition from education to work and between jobs.

In some countries, collaboration among the stakeholders has worked well when discussions are articulated around clear objectives and realistic time tables. In Estonia, working groups that involve several ministries have been successful when they address short-term and concrete skills issues. In the Netherlands, collaboration across regional/sub-regional administrative levels has proven successful when there has been a process for them to mutually agree on the policy objectives while leaving flexibility to local administrations to implement them under realistic time frames. Setting specific objectives and policy priorities has helped inter-ministerial collaboration in the United States as has the consistency of participant to these inter-ministerial working groups.

Conclusions

This chapter identified three different models for the governance of skills assessment and anticipation exercises, depending upon how closely their existence is tied to a specific policy objective. In the independent model, skills assessment and anticipation exercises are led by independent agencies and they are not designed for a single, narrow policy use. Instead, exercises run under this model follow the spirit of general labour market information systems, in that they provide a general tool for policy making and the development of the exercise is independent of the end users of the information produced. By contrast, in the policy model of governance, end users of the information are also those who lead the exercise, and the exercise is directly linked to specific policies or programmes. A third approach, the hybrid model, lies in between these two: exercises are led by agencies with clear policy objectives, but their design and development is relatively independent of a particular and specific policy use.

The governance of skills assessment and anticipation exercises is important because poor governance may limit the potential usefulness of the exercises. In the "policy model", skills assessment and anticipation exercises are directly linked to specific policy uses. This may be considered as positive in that the information produced is exactly the information required by the users; it is more likely to result in evidence-based policy. On the downside, exercises developed under this governance model are less likely to be of more general use because of their narrow focus. Under the policy model, there is also a risk of proliferation of exercises and, therefore, of wasteful duplication. In fact, in many countries, the existence of large numbers of exercises is identified as a barrier hindering dialogue and policy making – particularly where they are not harmonised or lead to conflicting messages. In this respect, efforts are being carried out in a few countries to establish networks, or consolidate different assessment and anticipation exercises, in the hope of better co-ordinating the production and use of information.

In the "independent" model, an independent body carries out the exercise (e.g. the statistical office) and the policy uses are not pre-defined. This model legitimises the information produced on skills needs (since they are independent) and the information is also meant for much wider use. This approach may, however, face the barrier that some of the potential users are not aware of the information, or that the instrument is not aligned to their needs. This barrier is overcome in several countries by involving potential users in the governance or the development of the exercise. This barrier is overcome in other countries by involving the analysts carrying out the exercises in the policy development process.

Stakeholder involvement in skills assessments and anticipation exercises can, in general terms, also take one of two forms. A more informal mechanism involves stakeholders on an *ad-hoc* basis. Such involvement can be based on a long-standing tradition of stakeholder collaboration (or not). Alternatively, more formal approaches to collaboration include the participation of different stakeholders in the governance of a specific agency responsible for skills policy (e.g. advisory boards to ministries, membership in agencies governing VET systems) or in the governance of the skills assessment and anticipation exercise itself. Involving stakeholders in the agency that carries out the exercises can help build a common understanding of long-term skills needs and also make sure that the design of the exercise is more aligned to the objectives of each specific user. This mechanism of co-ordination does not ensure, however, consensus or even stakeholder involvement in the development of a policy response. *Ad-hoc* meetings can also be successful because they focus the discussion on a specific issue – although they may lack regularity and constancy in participants across different working groups. Leading discussions with stakeholders around specific objectives promotes successful dialogue, though it requires an agency defining these objectives and priorities, and also that there is consensus on the priority-setting mechanism and the objectives to be achieved across the stakeholders.

Whatever the mechanism in place to facilitate and co-ordinate stakeholder involvement, it works best when social partners are represented by strong organisations that represent the sectoral interests and the majority of their constituency. It also works best when inter-ministerial or stakeholder involvement counts with strong political engagement from government agencies, across regional/sub-regional administrative levels and from within the social partners. This engagement is facilitated when stakeholders find individual benefits to collaboration and when they feel their input is necessary for an accurate discussion of results and effective policy development. Also, the presence of a skills strategy can frame discussions around the results from skills assessment and anticipation exercises and the ensuing policy response. Legislation regulating the forms and modes of collaboration can also help, but needs to be enforced.

Note

1. The European "open method of co-ordination" is another example of bringing about co-operation in a multi-level structure towards certain commonly agreed goals and objectives (see CEDEFOP, 2008). Also, a multi-level governance framework has been formulated by the OECD and has been used in several areas of work related to multi-level governance including on Public investment, regional development, urban development, local finances, water governance, regulatory policy or environmental issues such as climate change.

References

Andersen, T. et al. (2010), "Anticipating Skill Needs of the Labour Force and Equipping People for New Jobs, Which Role for Public Employment Services in Early Identification of Skill Needs and Labour Up-Skilling?", Final report prepared under contract to the European Commission, Directorate General for Employment, Social Affairs and Equal Opportunities.

Bartlett, W. (2013), "Structural Unemployment in the Western Balkans: Challenges for Skills Anticipation and Matching Policies", *European Planning Studies*, Vol. 21, No. 6, pp. 890-908.

Blázquez, M. (2014), *Skills-Based Profiling and Matching in PES*, Publications Office of the European Union, Luxembourg.

CEDEFOP (2008), "Systems for Anticipation of Skill Needs in the EU Member States", *CEDEFOP Working Paper*, Vol. 1.

Commission of the European Communities (2009), *New Skills for New Jobs: Anticipating and Matching Labour Market and Skills Needs*, COM(2008) 868 Final, Brussels.

European Commission (2013), "Peer Review on Performance Management in Public Employment Services (PES)", Copenhagen, March.

European Commission (2010), *New Skills for New Jobs: Policy Initiatives in the Field of Education*, Education, Audiovisual and Culture Executive Agency, Brussels.

Froy, F. et al. (2011), "Building Flexibility and Accountability into Local Employment Services: Synthesis of OECD Studies in Belgium, Canada, Denmark and the Netherlands", *OECD Local Economic and Employment Development (LEED) Working Papers*, No. 2011/10, OECD Publishing, Paris, http://dx.doi.org/10.1787/5kg3mkv3tr21-en.

Manoudi, A. et al. (2014), *EEPO Small Case Study on PES Business Models*, European Commission, Brussels.

McCarthaigh, M. (2013), *The Changing Structure of Irish Sub-National Governance*, Institute of Public Administration, Dublin.

Nurmela, K. (2011), *Social Partnership for Anticipating Change in the Labour Market: National Paper Estonia*, Praxis Center for Policy Studies, Tallinn.

OECD (2015), *OECD Skill Strategy Diagnostic Report: Portugal*, OECD, Paris, https://skills.oecd.org/developskills/documents/Portugal-Diagnostic-Report-web.pdf.

OECD (2014), *Job Creation and Local Economic Development*, OECD Publishing, Paris, http://dx.doi.org/10.1787/9789264215009-en.

Annex A
Responses to the questionnaire

The questionnaire was sent to the Ministry of Education, the Ministry of Labour, employer organisations and trade union confederations in all OECD countries. The table below shows the number of replies to the questionnaire received from each country.

Table A.1. **Number of replies to the questionnaire on anticipating and responding to changing skill needs**

	Ministry of Labour	Ministry of Education	Employer organisation	Union confederation
Australia	1	0	0	0
Austria	1	1	0	0
Belgium	3	1	0	0
Canada	1	0	2	0
Chile	1	1	1	0
Czech Republic	1	0	1	0
Denmark*	1	0	2	1
Estonia*	1	0	0	0
Finland	1	1	1	1
France*	1	0	1	2
Germany	1	1	0	1
Greece	1	0	1	0
Hungary	0	1	0	0
Ireland	0	1	1	1
Iceland	0	0	0	0
Israel	0	0	0	0
Italy	0	1	0	0
Japan	1	0	2	0
Korea	1	0	1	0
Luxembourg	0	0	0	0
Mexico	0	0	0	0
Netherlands	1	0	1	0
Norway	1	1	1	1
New Zealand	0	0	0	0
Poland	1	0	0	0
Portugal*	1	1	0	0
Spain	0	1	1	2
Slovak Republic	1	0	1	0
Slovenia	1	0	1	1
Sweden	1	1	0	1
Switzerland	1	0	0	0
Turkey*	1	1	0	1
United Kingdom	0	0	0	1
United States	1	0	0	0

* The Danish and Estonian Ministries of Education responded to the Labour Questionnaire. France's Ministries of Education and Labour responded jointly to the Labour Questionnaire. A Portuguese large employer responded to the questionnaire but not in relation to skills assessment and anticipation exercises, but in relation to its internal skill management policies; the response was not considered in the report. Turkey's public employment service responded to a previous version of the questionnaire. Its content is reflected in the draft and the examples provided, but not included in the calculation of tables or figures.

StatLink http://dx.doi.org/10.1787/888933334068

ORGANISATION FOR ECONOMIC CO-OPERATION AND DEVELOPMENT

The OECD is a unique forum where governments work together to address the economic, social and environmental challenges of globalisation. The OECD is also at the forefront of efforts to understand and to help governments respond to new developments and concerns, such as corporate governance, the information economy and the challenges of an ageing population. The Organisation provides a setting where governments can compare policy experiences, seek answers to common problems, identify good practice and work to co-ordinate domestic and international policies.

The OECD member countries are: Australia, Austria, Belgium, Canada, Chile, the Czech Republic, Denmark, Estonia, Finland, France, Germany, Greece, Hungary, Iceland, Ireland, Israel, Italy, Japan, Korea, Luxembourg, Mexico, the Netherlands, New Zealand, Norway, Poland, Portugal, the Slovak Republic, Slovenia, Spain, Sweden, Switzerland, Turkey, the United Kingdom and the United States. The European Union takes part in the work of the OECD.

OECD Publishing disseminates widely the results of the Organisation's statistics gathering and research on economic, social and environmental issues, as well as the conventions, guidelines and standards agreed by its members.

OECD PUBLISHING, 2, rue André-Pascal, 75775 PARIS CEDEX 16
(81 2016 04 1 P) ISBN 978-92-64-25206-6 – 2016

www.ingramcontent.com/pod-product-compliance
Lightning Source LLC
LaVergne TN
LVHW081417110826
845149LV00010B/1780
* 9 7 8 9 2 6 4 2 5 2 0 6 6 *